Prison \

2001

Jul
ed:
ma
Ne

La
En
lor
sin

evious
justice
to *The*

en an
vith a
Vriting

Prison Writing 2001

Edition No. 15

Published November 2000 by
WATERSIDE PRESS
Domum Road
Winchester SO23 9NN

Telephone or Fax: 01962 855567
E-mail: watersidepress@compuserve.com
Online catalogue and bookstore: www.watersidepress.co.uk

ISBN 1 872 870 87 2

Catalogue-In-Publication Data: A catalogue record for this book can be obtained from the British Library

Printing and binding: Antony Rowe Ltd, Chippenham

Cover design: John Good Holbrook Ltd, Coventry

Cover artwork: Peter Cameron. Peter Cameron started painting whilst serving a ten and a half year prison sentence and came to terms with his imprisonment by making it the subject of his art. He is now a freelance artist working from Liverpool (The Hub, 9-13 Berry Street, Liverpool: Telephone 0151 709 0889). His story is one of several told in *Going Straight* (Waterside Press, 1998).

Entries for future editions: People wishing to submit material with a view to publication should write direct to

> The Editors
> Prison Writing
> PO Box 478
> Sheffield S3 SYX

Contributions whether fact, fiction, verse or other forms of writing are welcome from prisoners and other people connected to prisons in the United Kingdom or anywhere in the world. They may be on any subject. All contributors whose work is published automatically receive two complimentary copies of the edition of *Prison Writing* containing their entry and a nominal payment.

Prison Writing

Edited by

Julian Broadhead and Laura Kerr

2001

No. 15

WATERSIDE PRESS
WINCHESTER

Foreword

Twelve months ago *Prison Writing* looked dead and buried. Seven years and 14 issues since it began, the effort of editing and producing a hundred page journal every six months, as well as publicising, selling it and sticking stamps on envelopes—all in their spare time— had become too much for the humble editor, his assistant and occasional helpers.

The response to the journal's demise was loud and long; we received more correspondence after the last issue than we had over several years. Then, out of the blue, and largely as a result of a brief comment in *The Guardian*, along the lines of 'Prison Writing should not be allowed to die', Waterside Press came along. The result is this book, which it is hoped will become an annual publication.

The contents here feature as wide a range of writing by prisoners as is likely to be found anywhere. For many of the contributors it is their first time in print, several others have been in the old *Prison Writing* and a few of those are more widely published. A variety of topics are covered, fact and fiction and verse, in the main—but not all-prison-related. The majority of the contributors are in British prisons, but there are some too from America, Australia and Thailand. The international aspect is something we are keen to develop as time goes on.

Once this issue has begun to circulate, a publicity campaign to encourage material for the next one will begin—but, as ever, we welcome material, either direct from prisoners or from those with responsibility for their interests.

Read on.

Julian Broadhead
Laura Kerr

Editors

November 2000

Prison Writing CONTENTS

Looking Back

From Future to Past

Reviews

The *Prison Writing* Interview

Noel 'Razor' Smith was first published in the second issue of *Prison Writing*, in 1992. One of his poems, *Old Lags*, was picked up soon afterwards as *The Independent's* Daily Poem and his work has subsequently appeared in many newspapers and magazines, as well as being read on BBC Radio 4. In 1998 he was released on parole from a 19 year sentence but the following year was arrested for armed robberies and subsequently sentenced to life imprisonment under the two-strikes law. While on remand in Belmarsh, he wrote two articles about Jonathan Aitken, which were published in *Punch* and reported widely in the mainstream press. After printing so much of his work in *Prison Writing* over the past eight years, we thought readers might like to know more about Razor Smith. Interviewed while in Belmarsh by *PW* editor, Julian Broadhead, Razor has since been transferred to Whitemoor.

JB *To start at the very beginning, before you ever began to write you taught yourself to read and write in Borstal . . .*

RS Yes, in Rochester in 1977. I was 16. When I got there I could write my name but I had only the most basic grasp of reading and writing. Educationally, I was a six-year-old. At Christmas '77 I attempted an escape from the new 'escape-proof' wing and ended up cracking a night watchman's skull with a steel mop bucket. I was charged with causing gross personal violence to an officer. And attempted escape. As I was not a borstal trainee, but a detainee under the CYP Act 1933, Section 53(2).[1] I couldn't lose remission as I didn't have any. So I was sentenced to indefinite solitary confinement.

I was allowed one book a week and that was the full extent of the entertainment on offer. A Roman Catholic priest came to the block to see me and saw that I was struggling to read my Alistair McClean allowance, so he brought me a couple of *Janet and Johns*, and then left them with me. I had nothing else to do, so I cracked on with them and soon I was seeing 'Spot run'. Lousy plots in *Janet and John* and the endings are so predictable . . . Next he brought me a *Dr Seuss* and that was better. I've still got a soft spot for *The Cat in the Hat*, but I do not like green eggs and ham . . . I struggled through those books 20 times a day, saying the words out loud until I had them. The priest would drop in every now

---

[1] Children and Young Persons Act 1933. Section 53 deals with 'grave crimes' committed by juveniles—here 'A person under the age of 18 who has been sentenced for an offence that would warrant a sentence of 14 years or over in an adult'.

and again and ask me to read them out loud and tell me the words I was getting wrong. He asked the governor if I could have writing materials but he refused me a pencil as I had previous for sticking them into people, but he did let me have a crayon and paper.

After six months I had grasped enough to read a paperback and get through a simple letter. The first book I read all the way through was Alistair McClean's *Force 10 From Navarone*—it took me six weeks to finish. My mum said she cried when, after I'd been away for 16 months she got her first letter from me. I was in the block for nine months and by the time I came off punishment I could read and write as good as any 12-year-old.

JB *Where does the Razor nickname come from?*

RS I got the Razor tag when I became a teddy boy at the age of 14. A mate of mine was badly beaten by a gang of skinheads. They poured paint-stripper on him and set him alight. He nearly died. So I went to the club where they all hung out and charged in with a couple of big, old cut-throat razors and opened up everyone in the club. It was a proper bloodbath—I slashed everything that moved, including the DJ and two barmen. It made the local paper and I was nicked but everyone refused to give evidence, they all thought I was a nutter. From then on I was 'Razor' Smith and I played on it, learned a couple of fancy moves with a razor and perfected my 'mad stare'. The rest is history but I tell the full story in the book I'm writing, *The Last Party*.

JB *What is it about being in jail that makes men write?*

RS Boredom . . . the need to let the outside world, and yourself, know that you still exist—I create, therefore I am! Entertainment . . . to relieve frustration at the system. I know men who don't have the confidence to jot down a four line poem, but who will spend hours with a dictionary writing out a Request/Complaint form every single week. Some of them are works of art . . . Plus—there are not many creative things you can do from inside a cell with plenty of time on your hands.

JB *Is it a particular type of prisoner who writes?*

RS My theory is that most prison 'faces' are frustrated actors, glory-seekers and self-promoters. I include myself in that. We build a legend early on, maybe not intentionally at first, but you soon realise that every move contributes to the legend. We want people to know that we are not just ciphers, not part of the herd, and the more people that know, the better. Look at Valerio Viccei,[2] leaving his bloody thumbprint all over the Knightsbridge vault . . . If you're prepared to go that extra inch in crime or fighting the system, then you want credit for it, everyone does. We want self-esteem, respect, fame—or infamy, and if there's a bit of fortune on offer as well, all the better. Those of us who are able to write, do. Those who can't get Kate Kray or James Morton or someone else to do it for them.

Some people become criminals not only for the loot, but also because it's the only way open for them to make a mark on the world. Writing gives the prisoner power—if you get published, especially in a widely read publication, it makes the screws a bit more wary of you. Most of them have trouble filling in a nicking sheet. One thing the system hates is an educated con. When you think that 16 per cent of the prison population can't read and write at all, 48 per cent have minimal reading and writing skills, and a good proportion of the rest have little to say and no interest in writing it down.

There is plenty of other talent in jail—sculptors, painters, musicians, great sportsmen, world class chess and backgammon players. But with prison writers, I have also read stuff in jail that will never see the light of day because the people who've written it don't have the confidence to submit it. So the pool of prison writers is relatively small—and the ones that make it into print are the ego-driven madmen who have interesting stories to tell and who have a modicum of writing talent.

JB *Can you remember what first got you interested in writing?*

RS Reading led me directly to writing. Once I could read, I saw writing as the next logical step. Coming to it late, I didn't know any different, I thought everyone could do it. I started writing personalised funny poems for people. And then I read *The Villain's Tale* by G. F. Newman and I thought fuckin' hell! This geezer knows what it's all about! His books were 'floaters', banned by the borstal, but copies were smuggled in and from wing to wing. We used to rip the covers off them cos if you got caught with one it was seven days block. G. F. Newman gave me the idea that I might have some stories to put in writing. The rest of the books in borstal were all pre-1940s ex-navy stock. They were all stamped with the names of the ships they came from—loads of Agatha Christie and the

---

[2] Valerio Viccei was sentenced to 22 years in 1987 for the multi-million pound Knightsbridge Safe Deposit Co. robbery. He wrote a book while in HMP Parkhurst and was interviewed in *Prison Writing* in 1992, shortly before returning to Italy to serve his sentence. He died in a shoot-out with police near Rome in April 2000.

like. G. F. Newman wasn't afraid to say 'fuck' in print, and that brought writing down to my level.

JB *How much has what you've read influenced you?*

RS In the early days I would be influenced by whatever author I happened to be reading at the time. My writing would reflect their style. G. F. Newman and Damon Runyan were the big ones and I think you can see both of them in my short stories. I class Runyon as one of the funniest storytellers ever. John Steinbeck is also a great influence and has written a lot of funny stuff like *Tortilla Flat* and *Cannery Row*. I also remember a feeling of achievement when I finished reading James A. Michener's *Centennial*, a good book and over a thousand pages long. But I've read thousands of books—about five a week is average in jail and say 75 per cent of them are pure crap. I don't know how most of them get into print—which is encouraging because I think if rubbish can be published so easily then surely I can do better and be in with a chance. I've lost count of the number of books I've launched across the cell after a couple of chapters.

JB *What directs what you read?*

RS When I first learned to read I would read anything that was available. I've read the Bible four times when I've been down the block—I'm a born again atheist. Now I read mainly for entertainment, and to check out the opposition.

JB *Who are you writing for? Is it for yourself . . . your peers in or out of prison . . . to inform a wider public?*

RS I started writing for myself as a form of therapy. Then I wrote for other cons . . . poems etc. then after I was first published—in *Prison Writing No. 2*—I wrote for cons and the outside world. Then for my family and friends and now for anyone who will read it.

JB *Can you recall how it felt to see your work in print for the first time?*

RS When I first got *PW2* I was in a trance for six weeks! It took that long for it to sink in. I must have read it a thousand times and I showed it to everyone. The only thing that compared to it was being at the birth of my first son—it was such a buzz. Even at that stage I remember thinking that if I never had another word published I wouldn't mind because I had this. It was such a feeling of achievement, someone outside had paid me money and published my writing for everyone to read! It blew me away.

I can still get the exact feeling when I open *PW 2* and see my name in the contents. My copy was literally worn out, my mum has got it at home somewhere, yellowed, frayed and held together with Sellotape like an ancient holy relic.

JB *The first work you had printed was the poem 'Old Lags', which was later reprinted in 'The Independent'. What was the background to, the source of 'Old Lags'?*

RS I was just listening to the wing in Wandsworth one day and I suddenly realised how we all say the same things in greeting to each other. We always ask after other villains and laugh about our misfortunes because prison is such a macho world. I'd been having similar conversations for as long as I'd been inside yet now I was really only hearing them for the first time.

JB *How much do you feel censored by writing from within? Would your work be more critical if you were outside?*

RS I can honestly say that this is the first prison [*Belmarsh*] where I have been truly censored. Everything I send through the post is passed to security on the orders of the governor, copied, perused and passed around. I've lost count of the number of governors and security officers I've been called in front of over my letters and articles. But all they do is make me more determined. In fact, now that they have thrown the gauntlet down I dig them out all the more. I can't resist a challenge, it's part of my nature and what makes me what I am—and I genuinely detest the system. Fuck'em, if they can't take the truth—and I always make sure what I write is the truth. It goes back to the question about *who* I write for . . .

So now when I write I know who will be reading it first and it adds a splash of vitriol to the mix. I'm doing eight life sentences for nicking a few quid, so what can these people do to make it any worse? I've had beatings, been injected, and spent years of my life in punishment blocks and I've never expected any less from these people. Unless they kill me, they're out of luck. I'll keep on writing and surviving. One day at a time. So to the answer the question, no—my work couldn't be any more critical.

JB *Do you think that things will get easier in prison when the Human Rights Act starts to take effect? What is the feeling among prisoners about that?*

RS Cons are cautiously optimistic about the HRA but nobody is really sure if it will make any difference to us. Some cons think we'll get conjugal visits, no censorship of letters and phone calls, an end to the two-strikes life etc.

Things are so bad in jail now that cons are willing to grasp any hope of improvement as something to look forward to. It can't get much worse—unless of course the HRA makes no difference to our lives, then people will see riot as the only way to get a change. The last resort. I hope the HRA does something to put things right—if not there are going to be a lot of pissed off cons and I'll be one of them. The worst thing is not having any information.

JB *What are the main encouragements and main oppositions to writing seriously while in prison?*

RS The main encouragement to writing in jail is that you have the time to do it. Also, you re-live memories so often that you're aware of details, and thinking time is available. Plus, you affirm your existence by reaching the out—I'm not dead and buried because people who have never met me are out there reading my words. I'm entombed but I live !

The only opposition is the paranoid system.

JB *How much have education departments, teachers or writers in residence helped or encouraged your writing?*

RS Whenever I was inside I would get on Education, simply because it was a doss compared to the workshops. I kept on reading as it was a bird killer and the more I read the better I got at it. For a laugh I would write funny poems about people and incidents on the wing. I would also write to take out my frustrations at the system. A few cons saw my poems and I began to get the odd request for personalised ones. A quarter ounce of Old H would get you a sugary little six liner that you could send to your bird and pretend you'd done it yourself.

In 1992 I saw an advert in *Inside Time* for *Prison Writing* and sent some stuff off. I promptly escaped, and when I was recaptured I was sent to a brand new nick, Highdown, in Surrey. In the meantime my stuff had been published in *Prison Writing*—and that affected me more than the 15 years that was added to my sentence. I really got interested in writing then. Highdown had computers in the education department and when I realised you could write on them you couldn't prise me out of the education department with a crowbar.

I wrote funny, subversive poems and short articles under the pen name of The Outlaw, printed up loads of copies and distributed them around the jail. The stuff was really over the top, slagging screws and governors by name. Eventually a grass put me up and I was given the gypsy's warning by a P.O. and shipped out.

I came back to Highdown in '94, with a few more bits and pieces under my belt—*Prison Writing, The Independent, Passport Magazine* and a BBC Radio 4 interview for *Stanza*. Stephen Prior, who was the Number One Governor at Highdown, came to my cell and told me that he had heard my Radio 4 piece and was impressed. He made me a deal—he was willing to overlook my terrible prison record and not send me back to Dartmoor if I would keep out of trouble and start up a prison magazine. I jumped at the chance and as a result Mr. Prior and Eileen Jackman, the head of education, agreed to fund me for a diploma course in freelance feature writing with the London School of Journalism. I passed that with an honours diploma, one of only two handed out that year. So, to finally answer the question, with the exception of that priest in Rochester—to my shame, I never knew his name—the only prison that ever helped or encouraged me to write was Highdown. With the exception of the late John Marriott, Stephen Prior was the most enlightened, humane prison governor I have ever met. And believe me, I've stood in front of plenty of them.

Most other jails I've been in take an indifferent view of my writing. Belmarsh is the only one that has openly attacked and punished me for it. I didn't know the meaning of censorship until I came here.

JB *Last year you had a couple of pieces in 'Punch', about Jonathan Aitken being in a nearby cell. How did they come about?*

RS They say that every cloud has a silver lining and it certainly proved to be the case in the Jonathan Aitken coup. There I was, an aspiring writer with a journalism diploma under my belt, on remand for eight armed robberies in the most secure jail in the country, when along comes J. A. Talk about a Johnny-on-the spot—they put him in a cell two doors away from me! The media were having a feeding frenzy over him, but I was the only writer who could get within three hundred feet of the man. Before I met Aitken, the only person I had ever interviewed was Alan Minter, ex-middleweight champion of the world, for a prison magazine, so I didn't really have much of a clue, but being a blagger means that you've got to have plenty of front and bluff and that came in useful.

Aitken himself was brilliant about it. He answered almost every question I asked him. Amazing really when you think of his troubles with journos and how he came to be in Belmarsh in the first place. He wouldn't be drawn on Thatcher or her daughter, but everything else was no problem.

I've always classed myself as a bit of a left-wing-anarchist-liberal, if there is such a thing, and I detest the Tories and all they stand for, but as I got to know Aitken I began to like him. He really is a charming and likeable man, and he handled his time here very well. The stuff I did on him went to *Punch*, and of course all the nationals picked up on it. I had initially offered my first piece to *The Guardian*, thinking they would jump at the chance. I wrote to Nick Hopkins, who took over from Duncan Campbell as crime correspondent, but I didn't even get a reply. I had done quite a bit of work for them so I was surprised that when the first *Punch* article came out they sneered at me and 'thugged' me off in an editorial. I now read *The Times*.

J. A. is still in touch. I get a letter every month, which is more than I get from some friends who I have known all my life. He did an interview about his book in the *Sunday Times* a few months ago and my name came up. The interviewer described me as a 'hardened brute' and Johnny immediately wrote to apologise on her behalf. He says I'll have a whole chapter when he comes to write his prison memoirs, no doubt getting his own back for the *Punch* stuff!

JB *I'm surprised that you sent it to 'The Guardian', given their role in the whole Aitken episode . . .*

RS I was naïve enough to believe that once they had had their pound of flesh and utterly destroyed Aitken, they would be big enough to take the boot off his neck and say '. . . we've proved our point, now let's show how even handed we are.' It would have made them look fair, instead they crowed about what they had done, like a playground bully. I'd expect that from the *Sun*, but *The Guardian*? I mean, it's not as if my articles were uncritical of Aitken, I said some pretty nasty things about him. And there's the rub—Johnny Aitken could have just blanked me over it—but he's still in touch.

I'd like to put the Aitken thing in perspective from my point of view—he told a few lies, got his daughter to lie for him and took a bribe. For this he was made bankrupt, held in one of the most secure jails in Europe, pilloried in the press and held up to public ridicule. For almost every day of my life I have been surrounded by men who have raped and killed women, children and old aged pensioners; who would take your eye out or throw scalding water in your face for a £10 drug debt; who would think nothing of coshing an old woman for the contents of a cancer research charity box and a second class stamp. So to me Aitken's 'crimes' are about as small-fry as you can get.

That mob at *The Guardian* had a very good payday out of Aitken, what with the book, the free publicity and the court payout, so naturally I assumed they could afford to be magnanimous in their victory. Unfortunately that didn't prove to be the case and I was mistaken. C'est la vie !

JB *You mentioned the prison magazine, which was called 'Sorted', if I recall— and very different to the run-of-the-mill type that most prisons—if they bother at all—turn out. You wrote a lot of the content yourself...?*

RS *Sorted* ran for ten issues and won a Koestler award against some very stiff opposition. As I've said, it was a testament to the great attitude that Stephen Prior had in running his prison. He gave me access to three good computers, a photocopier and a printing press and just said 'Have a go.' So I did. It was a learning experience, every issue taught me something, and by No. 5 we had won the Koestler. I'm still very proud of *Sorted*, there has never been another prison mag like it. Mr Prior told me from the start that there would be no censorship by staff but if anyone made a complaint about the contents it would be up tó them to argue the validity. If any staff complained, and a few did, he would get us together to thrash it out, and if their complaint was upheld I would have to publish an apology in the next issue. This only happened twice.

I had a budget of £200 per issue and this allowed me to get a copy to every con in the jail, including the punishment block, and also offer prizes for the crossword and competition. Charlie Bronson was a regular contributor for a while, as was Clare Barstow, whose stuff you've often printed in *PW*. The hard work was getting enough contributors to hand in cartoons, stories, articles etc. on time. We got hundreds of poems though . . .

JB *I can believe it. We get thousands at Prison Writing!*

RS Sometimes three quarters of the issue would be written by me and co-editor Alex Begg, using different styles and names. Johnny Sansom, who did a *PW* cover, was our regular artist and cartoonist

JB *You got out from your last sentence in August 1998 and were about a year. How difficult was it to continue writing, outside.*

RS When I got out all I wanted to do was catch up on the life I'd missed. I couldn't find the time or the inclination to sit down and write. It's a much faster pace out there . . . I was glad to get out, but it all happened a bit sudden. I had no home leave, no pre-release preparation, no money, no clothes, nothing. I got released as a B cat. The DSS refused me a clothing grant, even for work clothes and they wanted to pay me £98 a fortnight. The only jobs I was suited for were labouring or sweeping the streets which I did for five months. I had that piece in the *New Law Journal* and some stuff in *The Guardian* and a bit of radio work but they are slow payers. It's all right when you're in jail with a cockle a week expenses, a cheque is money in the bank. But out there, when the money don't arrive it means another week of walking to work and living on cup-a-soup. I'm crap at managing money—I've got the typical blagger's mentality—spend it quick in case you get nicked and they claw it back. Easy come, easy go. It's hard for straight goers and even conventional criminals to understand the temptation of the experienced bank robber. When you're broke, it's always lurking in the back of your mind that you know the drill. You know you can stroll into any bank with your hand in a paper bag and walk out 90 seconds later with a couple of grand. I know it's a childish, immature, short-term solution, but it's there. And if you're used to having a few quid and spending it like a sailor, and then after a decade in shovel you find yourself sweeping the roads and living on toasted carpet three days a week, the temptation becomes a siren song. Course, once you've done one, that's it, you're off and running, hung for a sheep as a lamb etc. In that sort of situation, writing takes a back seat. But knowing you'll write again makes you take more notice of what's going on, future tales being researched in living colour.

JB *When you got out from that sentence, the novelist Will Self showed some interest in your work and recommended you to an agent. What happened there?*

RS I met him through John McVicar who interviewed me for *Punch* when I first got out. I gave him a copy of a short story, *The Reluctant Counterpuncher*, which was the last story I completed before I left prison. He showed it to Will Self and the next thing I know he's on the phone inviting me to dinner. He was very enthusiastic about my style of writing and arranged for me to meet his agent.

So I went to see the agent, a thirty-something woman who was far more at home dealing with 'proper writers' who had college educations and used six big words where one small one would do. It didn't help that I was driving my brother's work van, with Lambeth Council on the side and I got into a row outside her office with a traffic warden and threatened to kick him right in the bollocks if he put a ticket on the van.

She heard it all and to say my reception was cool is like saying that George Cornell died of lead poisoning. She insisted that if I wanted to become 'saleable' I would have to change my writing style. I said 'It's my style that got me the meeting with you in the first place!' Needless to say, she didn't take me on.

JB *I know you encourage other prisoners in their writing, because they send their work to PW and tell me. What advice do you have for anyone who is in prison and is wants to write?*

RS Use prison to help you improve yourself. Harness all the frustration, bitterness and hate that you are bound to feel about your predicament and how the system operates. Get it out of your head and heart and onto the paper. Believe me, it helps.

In the long run screws are more worried about cons writing complaints or articles that expose them to outside bodies than they are about a clump in the jaw. If there is one thing the system fears more than anything else it is an articulate, educated prisoner who can wield a pen. They are indoctrinated to believe we are all stupid, low life thugs, to de-humanise us and so make it easier to do their job. They use the rules against us every day, so we use the rules against them in return. Get educated, it frightens the life out of them!

JB *What are you working on right now?*

RS At the moment I'm writing a book about my experiences after I came out of Rochester and before I went back to serious crime. I was still a teenager and wanted to catch up on the years I had missed. I was also very bitter, very violent and a little bit deranged. Plus, I was a rockabilly, and so I formed a gang from some of the most violent psychotics on the rockabilly scene and attempted to beat the life out of every other teen gang in London. We were called the Balham Wildkatz and we fought, drank, danced and fucked our way through the close of the 1970s and into the 1980s.

There were gang fights with the punks, the skinheads, the mods, the soul boys, the squares and finally among ourselves. Some of the violence was horrific and it all ended up in a murder case eventually, but it's not all blood and severed arms. The violence, though an essential part of the story, is almost incidental to the humour, music and fashions of that time. When you think about it, 79-80 was the final party of the teenage sub-culture. We all appeared at the same time and overlapped for the first and probably the last time. There were Teddy Boys in the 1950s, Mods in the 60s, Skinheads in the late 60s and early 70s, Punk Rockers in the mid-70s, New Romantics in the early 80s and Rockabillies, Psychobillies, Soul Boys, Funksters and Disco-Squares—all fighting for a place at the last party.

Name a teenage sub-culture that has appeared on the scene since the new romantics had their 15 minutes of fame in the early 80s. There haven't been any. We were the real Generation X.

I got a bit carried away there, I thought I was working on the book. Anyway, the working title for it is *The Last Party*.

JB *What writing ambitions do you have for the future?*

RS I read an article about Robert Ludlum, the novelist, a couple of years ago, and he lives on an island in the Caribbean and does four hours writing a day. That's my ambition! I'd like to get *The Last Party* published and see it sell. After that I've got a few good ideas for novels, a play and then maybe finish my criminal years autobiography. Prison is a great place for getting the writing done, plenty of spare time. My dream is to earn enough at writing while I'm in here so that when I get out, in ten or 15 years time, I'll be set for whatever life is left. I don't fancy the idea of leaping over bank counters when in my 50s! I think I've proved I have a modicum of talent at the writing game and I've been lucky. Some people write all their lives and never get anything published. So if I put in the hours, maybe I'll get lucky again.

●   ●   ●

Extracts from:
The Last Party, A Memoir-in-Progress

Razor Smith

The Teddy Boy . . . a background

Hey Mr. Tailor don't get cute
What I want is a Teddy Boy suit,
Sky-blue jacket with velvet cuffs
You better work fast or I might get rough

The Teddy Boy was an English phenomenon who rose to prominence in the drab austerity of the early 1950s. A descendant of the wartime spiv and post war cosh boy, he was, on the whole, a flashily-dressed, violent petty criminal who adopted rock n' roll music as his own.

The Teddy Boy *was* the spiv and the cosh boy, only better dressed and able to dance. The Teds were a working-class subculture that borrowed its style of dress from the west-end dandies of the Edwardian era, hence the name. Their style of dress was the drape suit, with velvet collar and cuffs, brocade waistcoat, string tie, and thick-soled brothel-creepers or winklepicker boots. As a further salute to the Edwardian era, many Teds cultivated mutton-chop sideburns.

The Teds became connected with rock n' roll music in 1955, when Bill Haley and the Comets' *Rock Around the Clock* was first heard over the opening of the teen-rebellion flick *Blackboard Jungle*. The Teds caused riots in cinemas up and down the country by jiving in the aisles and then slashing and ripping out their seats when ordered to sit down. From 1955 onwards, the words Teddy Boy and violence seemed synonymous and were hardly out of the news, until the mods and rockers stole their mantle in the early 1960s. Cinema seat slashings, stabbings, coshings, dance-hall gang fights and race riots were the milieu of the Teddy Boy.

Against all odds and expectations, Teddy Boys were still a thriving subculture in the mid-1970s. In London at least this was partly due to the original Ted fathers of the 1950s passing the rock n' roll baton on to their children. Families like the Hogans of Battersea, the Ransomes of the Elephant and Castle and the Hassans of Wandsworth kept up a visible Ted presence and also supplied a new generation of Teds in their children. In some cases, being a Ted was hereditary. The original Teds kept the club scene alive at places like the Edwardian Club in Brixton, the Tennessee in Wimbledon, the Lyceum in the Strand and BobbySox in Wood Green.

When I first became a Ted, in 1975, one of the things I loved was the sense of belonging to an exclusive club. In my beige three-button drape suit with black velvet collar and cuffs and half-moon pockets, I stood out from the herd of long-haired, bell-bottomed, tie-dyed drabs who made up the majority of my peers. Old people would smile and nod at me in the street, or stop and tell me how good the 1950s were. I could give, and expect, instant friendship and loyalty to any Ted I happened to meet. And best of all, there was always someone ready to stick a pint in my under-age hand at the Ted pubs and clubs.

The downside was that Teds were easy to spot in a crowd and the police never tired of stopping and searching us for weapons.

But the worst thing about the Teds was that it wasn't only their music and style of dress that harked back to the 50s, but in a lot of cases their attitudes as well. They were notoriously racist, fervently patriotic and uncompromising monarchists. One of the few things that could stop a cinema-seat slasher in full swing was the opening bars of *God Save the Queen*.

In fact, one of the reasons for the great Ted vs. Punk battles of 1978 was because the Sex Pistols had recorded a piss-take version of the national anthem and many punk rockers were wearing pictures of HM on their tee-shirts with a safety pin through her nose. This offended the sensibilities of the ultra-royalist Teds, who suddenly became the darlings of the right-wing press and were hailed (or should that be heilled?) by the National Front for their attacks on punks.

...and then came Rockabilly

By the long, hot summer of 1976, the style of the 1950s was once more coming into vogue amongst teeenagers, due in part to films such as *American Graffiti* and *Lemon Popsicle*, and a popular American TV show called *Happy Days*, whose hero, 'The Fonz', was the epitome of the 50s bad-boy cool. The new breed of young rockers coming onto the scene classed the originals as little more than old duffers stuck in a time-warp, with their lime-green socks and Connie Francis LPs. What self-respecting teenager wants to wear the same clothes his parents wore? Personally, I was willing to become part of the new order, but not to desert the 1950s completely; we needed something new, to us at least, and yet essentially rooted in the rock n' roll decade. Rockabilly was it.

For the originals, the advent of rockabilly into their pubs and clubs was the biggest upset since Buddy's plane went down in '59. But it happened so quickly they were too surprised to put up any resistance. The winds of change began when an obscure 1954 rockabilly track, 'Jungle Rock' by Hank Mizzell, came out of nowhere and reached number one in the national pop charts, and they swept, zephyr-like, through an entire subculture. Most of the Teds were blown away. Rockabilly had arrived.

. . . the look

The first attempt by British teens to create a look to match the music is credited to the West London gangs and in particular, Scotty Johnson. Scotty, a one-time Teddy Boy and member of the Chiswick Flyers gang, figured that as rockabilly was performed mainly by rural labourers and farm boys, the look should reflect this. Check shirts, neckerchief, faded jeans or dungarees, steel-toe boots and donkey jacket, became the official uniform of the Rockabilly Rebel, for a while. If you've a mind to see Scotty Johnson in full outfit, then try to get hold of a 1978 LP on the Charly label called 'Rockabilly Rules OK'. The cover features a full colour picture of Scotty giving a clenched fist salute at the gates of Buckingham Palace. The Teds were incensed.

The Scotty Johnson look had its advantages, but it wasn't much cop for impressing the girls, unless their standards were particularly low. I once went to a girlfriend's house to pick her up for a night out, resplendent in my donkey jacket and boots, and overheard her father exclaimed—'I thought he'd come from the council to fix the drains.'

. . . out of jail and in the gang

The hangout was a ground-floor flat in Poynder Gardens. I don't know where the Gardens bit came in, 'cos Poynders was a rough old concrete and brick estate without a flower to its name. It was the sort of estate where if you didn't have a facial scar, the locals would think you were a copper. Every second car on the estate was stolen and being stripped for parts. Gangs of tattooed men, women, and children were feverishly wielding socket sets with a speed and dexterity that would be the envy of a Formula One pit stop mechanic.

As I walked out onto the estate I could hear Johnny Restivo giving it his all on 'The Shape I'm In', at full blast and I knew that was the flat I was looking for. I followed the sound past the burned-out social club and through a Cortina graveyard until I caught sight of the flat. All the windows were wide open and a confederate battle flag was rippling gently from one. There was no breeze at all, so it must have been the bass from the speaker that was making it ripple. It stopped about 20 feet away from the window and began to bop to the beat, my steels raising dust from the dry ground. The record came to an end, the flag stopped rippling and once again I could hear the faint clang of socket wrench on nut.

'Oi!' I shouted in the relative quiet. 'Turn that shit off and stick some Johnny Rotten on, you greasers!' My shout had the desired effect. From inside the flat came a rebel yell and three bods emerged through the window with all the panache of Errol Flynn in a pirate epic. The first one was shirtless and had red hair. He was carrying a small campers axe. This was Mad Harry. The last time I'd seen him he was a soul boy, marching the yard at Dover Borstal, that that had been over two years before. Now he had a greasy quiff, and was wearing drainpipe jeans and commando boots, the jeans held up with a Triumph sign buckle. We were best pals and had grown up together. The other two I didn't know, but they were similarly attired and swinging bike chains.

I held my hands out: 'What, only three of you?' I said. Harry's face broke into a huge grin. He threw the axe down and whooped as he grabbed me in a bear hug and swung me round. 'You cunt ! When did you get out?' The other two looked bemused as Harry patted me on the back and asked more questions than the flying squad. I looked up and saw three or four girls were now hanging out the windows of the flat. Harry turned to them. 'This is Razor. Rocky Mick's brother. He's been inside for fucking years. Look at him.'

...time for action

I was fired up and eager to throw a few digs and I didn't care who I threw them at. But I could see that what we were lacking was organisation. We needed a solid base, unity was the key. I had a few ideas, but they would have to wait until I'd met everyone. Some of these geezers didn't know me from a hole in the ground, so I couldn't just come along and take over. I would bide my time and embark on a 'hearts and minds' campaign. I would let them get to know me and what I was capable of, before giving any orders. My aim was to mould them into a crack fighting unit. More than that, a brotherhood. By the time I was finished we would be the most feared gang in London. I couldn't wait.

Of course, I know now that my years in Rochester, Dover and Ashford and Send had fucked me up. Violence became my voice and I used it to rage against the system. I became addicted to the burst of adrenalin high, in much the same way some people become addicted to heroin or cocaine. I knew it could get me killed or seriously injured, but I didn't care, I needed my fix of 'fuck the consequences' like a junkie needs his gear. And when I was released I still needed my fix. The borstal system had beaten me because the screws had a bigger gang than me. I had been on my own. But now I was going to have a gang and give back some of the hurt I had been given. My blood, my innocence and a good portion of my youth had fallen on the cold stone floors of punishment blocks. Now it was payback time.

The girls returned from their shopping trip and it was wine, women and song once more. Elaine took her place on my lap once again. Harry put on a Bill Haley LP and the whole flat was full of jiving couples. Dennis sat on the arm of a chair with a bottle of Olde English Cider in his mitt. I could see he was half cut already and the bottle was still three quarters full.

'What was it like inside?' he asked. I tried to shrug, but Elaine was nibbling my ear. What could I say to him? Could I tell him about my cellmate in Latchmere who tied a sock round his arm to cut off the flow of blood to his wrist before cutting it? How the paper-white skin made a ripping sound as he opened it up with a broken light-bulb? Or how desperately helpless and claustrophobic I felt when I was put in the straitjacket? Or how I opened up a north London kid's face with a razor blade melted into a toothbrush, because someone said he was in for rape. How could I explain the utter, hopeless, black despair I felt in the dark days and nights of solitary confinement? How I had yearned so much for freedom, I had actually tried to call the Devil up to trade my soul for an hour outside the walls? I looked at Dennis's young face and knew he would never spend one day in jail, no matter what I said. He wasn't the type, and he didn't even realise how lucky he was. I gave him a grin. 'It was just like *Jailhouse Rock*', I said, 'but without the singing and dancing.' He took a mouthful of cider and nodded. 'Yeah. That's what I thought,' he said.

. . . injun country

Going to visit Mad Harry in the Scrubs was a performance. But he was one of our own, and while he was in a London nick it was a point of honour that we visit him. Unfortunately it was also a point of honour that we fly our colours on the expeditions. To reach Hammersmith, in west London, where the Scrubs is situated, we had to pass through the badlands of enemy territory all the way. And, we had to go by tube.

The London tube system in 1979, was one of the favourite daytime haunts of glue-sniffing punk rockers and various other jobless, trouble-seeking teenage misfits like ourselves. Between rush-hours the trains were mainly empty and the stations all but deserted. A perfect canvas for the thug-as-artist to daub his mark. And in '79 there was no CCTV.

We walked straight past the ticket-collector at Balham station, Popeye casually flipping him the finger when he began to bluster after us. To us, paying on the tube was like plucking your eye out 'cos it offends you; stupid and unnecessary. Only squares and posh kids paid on the tube. Popeye sat on the hand-rail of the escalator and slid full-speed to the bottom. Me and Hollywood stayed on the moving staircase and watched the adverts go by. Hollywood was my latest squeeze. A short, pretty blonde with an hourglass figure and the IQ of a goldfish. She wore more make-up than Adam Ant, but that was only because she worked on the cosmetics counter of Woolworth's in Tooting Broadway and got it for nothing. She had ambitions to become a model, but I figured that being only five foot three would prove to be a bit of a handicap in the modelling game. When I mentioned this she got all pouty and rebuffed my advances for a couple of hours, so I kept my gob shut from then on. Why complicate things?

Hollywood looked like a typical Rockin' Chick, short blonde hair, bright red lipstick, chewing-gum, pencil skirt, white stilettos, and wearing Mad Harry's leather jacket, which was much too big for her. Bringing Harry's leather through injun country to the prison was an act of symbolism. We were showing him that, even though he was jailed, he was still a brother and we were flying his colours and keeping the faith. It would be kept safe for when he got out.

There was also a reason for taking Hollywood on such a dangerous mission, it was traditional to bring a female on a prison visit, as in those less enlightened times a con could go many months without catching a hint of perfume or seeing a well-turned ankle. It would make a nice change for Harry to see a girl. And Hollywood was sex-on-legs.

The platform was deserted so me and Hollywood got into a spit swapping contest, while Popeye broke open a chocolate machine and stuffed his pockets with Bar-Six, and Fruit and Nut. The tube soon rushed the station, pushing a tide of fetid air before it, and we boarded an empty carriage. We flopped down under a 'Please Do Not Put Your Feet On The Seats' sign, and put our feet on the seats.

The first bit of excitement came, as we had planned, at Clapham Common station, which was a notorious hangout for punks. As the tube pulled in we slipped our bike-chain belts off and got ready for action. There were a dozen punk rockers sprawled on the station benches drinking cider from the bottle and sniffing glue. As the tube door slid open, me and Popeye launched ourselves at them. They were caught completely unawares, we were in among them, kicking and flailing like a pair of lunatics. Popeye wrapped his chain around a spiky, multi-coloured head and threw a headbutt into another. I swung my steel toe-cap into a soft body mass and flicked my bike-chain at a punk who had been in the act of raising a cider bottle to his lips. The bottle shattered, cutting his hands and face. I swung my chain overhand and caught another across the shoulders as he tried to flee. The punks scattered and ran up the platform.

'Meet the WILDKATZ!' I shouted at the top of my voice. You get a really good echo in a tube station.

Time . . .

Time . . .

There are many reasons why prisoners write and send in their work to be considered for publication. For the author of this exploration into time and space in a small world that becomes smaller, it was less about being visited by the muse and more about threat. W. Maree writes from Coldingley: 'Innocent As Sin is the only story of mine based on a prison theme and the only story I have sent anywhere; and that only because a friend dragged me to a *Prison Writing* poster and told me he would throw me out the window if I did not submit something.'

Innocent As Sin

W. Maree

Time. It's all about time. A time to punish, punished by time; especially that second hand with the mean left hook. They let you keep a watch so you can discover all 86,400 seconds of a day without burdening the art of multiplication. After a while even the body becomes interesting. You delve for green delicacies, incessantly scratch a certain crevice—you'd be amazed at the variety of goo you never knew your body produced. It doesn't take long for these physical examinations to become as natural as disappearing in front of the telly when the wife mentions D-I-Y. The female of the species laboured for thousands of years to rid its males of this anti-social habit. Sadly the inert nature of 300-year-old bars has the knack of negating the finer touches of evolved propriety.

At this stage you start playing cards. With the cards come the unfortunate discoveries. That's what this is about, discoveries. I blame Socrates and Freud; you'll see why soon enough.

I have to begin with time's most esteemed hypothesis; the misconception we have come to call Evolution. We are told that Evolution takes time, a lot of it. This is where theory digresses slightly from the truth. Prison fact: millions of years of Evolution can be reversed in exactly one minute forty-three seconds, with five more seconds for the final transition.

Confused? Allow me to explain. One minute after the melting bag of flab opposite you carefully exposes his killer hand, you realise you are fondling your last, precious split matchstick. Forty-three seconds later an irresistible craving for the tobacco stained roll-up fag you've stashed above the ear kicks in. In the final seconds the last of your fire-making ability sputters into life and dies between a pair of digits that have been given a prudent coat of thick earwax. With the first cancer-ridden breath the homo-sapien in you spirals swiftly past the beginnings of civilisation and you are instantly touching on simian.

'Play again?' the giant molasses drones.

● ● ●

Priceless smoke pours from my mouth, 'You want my socks Al?' As a marketing man I realise this proposal is in need of a sales pitch, 'Prison issue, rarely washed, complement a skunk's backside; precious as hell.'

He sets his watery eyes on me. Some people say eyes are the windows to the soul. If that's the case, Al's soul closed shutters and ran years ago. His eyes were how I discovered that prison has a way of contradicting contemporary scientific belief. It was those eyes that allowed me to experience the quirk in evolution for the first time. I may speak primate now, but when they first slammed the one-sided door, those eyes wandered toward me and it was bye bye monkey, hello squirmy little slug thing. Real criminals have that effect on judicial misconceptions like myself.

He is considering the socks. He isn't blinking, so he must be thinking. 'Hmm,' his gut finally gurgles. He shifts a few matches in my direction. Big softy really. Good as currency speculation.

'Pay me back canteen day.'

Tighter than a falsetto's underpants. Then again, in the dumping ground of social surgery, nothing's free. You want a second-hand tea bag, it'll cost you the fermenting apple you've kept because you come from a country where nobody's heard of, let alone seen, black fruit.

'Okay, deal!' I tap the wobbly table.

It's been a strange day. Not strange as in different, that would unsettle the prison experience irrevocably, rather strange as in warped. I suspect last night's reading material is impinging on reality. Even fair England is playing along; you know things are not as they should be when an entire country is diligently contradicting itself. It's hot. I know, I know, you think I'm lying. Personally, I thought it was one of my post-traumatic hallucinations. Al's sobering presence is, however, always irrefutable, especially the way his body declares heat. Proof seeps from the robust, well-insulated muscles. The water he constantly sips from his plastic mug speeds through unseen (though quite audible) processes, is converted into an odorous toxic slime and pushed out of his pores in a stream of panicking blackheads. Even the halo of smoke clings to the atmosphere at a respectable distance. I opened the window earlier in the belief that my lungs were healthier than they felt. The institutionalised content of the cell still isn't interested in disturbing the fresh air.

Al's thick fingers slosh across his forehead. He starts to deal, marking the cards with the slick.

'You know,' I say, holding a fatal drag, 'First day I moved in I thought you were gonna jump me.'

'How you mean?' he asks, sorting his cards.

'You know,' I breathe the words in, willing my lungs to suck up every last microgram of precious nicotine, 'like prison,' I exhale, 'smaller cute guy gets doubled up with big, . . .' I make a strategic decision to omit the ugly, 'you know!'

'Na.'

'You know, the movies, about prisons . . . '

'Ah, yea . . . ' he throttles, reinforcing his words with one of the negative burps my nose has grown immune to.

'Glad it's not like that.' I smile.

His brain numbing expression drifts from his cards to me. 'What makes you think you're cute, huh?'

Now, I don't know about you, but when someone makes a crack like that, I expect him to smile, grin or even just smirk. Al's eyelids don't even twitch. My buttocks clench, I grin innocently, praying for the continued bliss of my virginity.

'You betting?' Facial movement. Thank you, thank you.

I push a match into the centre. My relieved gaze shifts toward my bunk. A beam of sunlight clashes with a visible atmosphere. This is where Socrates and Freud lie enraptured, basking in their personal aurora borealis. You are wondering what the creator and observer of modern madness are doing on my bed? To explain why I went where no sane man would, we have to explore the penal mutations of time and space.

When you are crammed into a barred sardine can with an obese cellmate, ticks flee. If any adverse tocks have offended a judge, I haven't found them. Time becomes a single unit, the infamous second hand that's given up the struggle to 12. In other words, it's like being dead, only you can still feel pain and, on cabbage days, smell.

Then it happens. You can't help it, no matter how stupid you are; your thoughts expand. Don't ask me why this happens. I can't explain it. I suspect the whispering toilet in the corner has something to do with it. Well, the morsels of consideration do spout; often germinating unto the walls as tiny squiggles of inspiration, livening your spirit, and then getting you nicked for vandalism. In the first months the primary reason for this neural wig wash is your crime.

Ah, now you wonder why I am here? It was a small case of opportune ignorance. How was I to know smuggling the icon of the peace and free-love movement in a totally ingenious, non-violent way, having never stolen, cheated and only rarely verbally abused another man, would cause such offence?

I will convince any man in debate of the perfect justifiability of my unreasonably illegal end. 'Hold up!' you say. 'The Judge? The jury?' I said man. They weren't human. So here I am, a victim of an inconvenient illegality squeezed into a claustrophobic rectangle with a real criminal and oracle toilet. Well, this is the price I pay for attempting to ship an entire sixties revival into a country where baggy-eyed, wet-nosed customs officers have large sensitive snouts.

'What you thinking about?' Al revs, trying to start another conversation, picking up three new cards from the lubricated pack.

'Monkeys and dogs.' I paraphrase.

He nods gravely, absorbing my profound revelation of self. But I divert. You don't speak about yourself when Socrates is drawing mazes in your head and Freud has comfortably tucked himself in under the belt. I excavated these two from a layer of arachnid art on a library shelf marked 'Other Stuff.' The shelf is really easy to find. All you have to do is ask the librarian if there is a section not marked 'Crime Fiction'.

Thing is, I wanted to know what it meant to be a criminal. To do this I had to find out how to blast the info out of Al's . . . well, let's call it mind for the sake of argument. So, armed with my newly acquired, totally sound philosophical-psychoanalytic skills I decided to hone in on Al's murky psyche.

'What did you feel when you pulled the trigger Al?' I ask, twirling the fag between two fingers.

He shuffles his cards around and scowls. Has a good hand again. 'It was kinda stiff. Mechanism needed oiling. You want to stroke the trigger, not yank it.'

The Freud suggested something I would rather not elaborate on; then turned its vicious suggestiveness to the fag in my hand; I stuck it in my mouth, giving it a good suck, the suggestiveness suddenly bordered on the perverse.

'No, I mean, how did you see the guy? How did you feel about him?'

'You playing or what?' he dumps a few more sticks into the pot.

I did the same, 'Come on Al. I'm curious.' The therapeutic suspension is killing me.

He raises an eyebrow, 'Sure you want to know what I saw?'

'Yea.'

'Look in a mirror.'

Okay, don't panic. Try to remember how the heart works.

He grunts a laugh. 'What is it I told you was most important in the gaff?'

I manage to squeeze a breath into my constricted lungs, 'Number One's all that counts, I think.'

'Yea,' he nods, rearranging his cards, 'Number One's all. Out on the street nothing's different. Friends'll run you down chase'n the dragon, or split you up 'n sell you for a rock. Money's all's matters. Money's what looks after you. Everybody out there's just walking meat with money stuck on like skin. More's got, the thicker's his skin, the harder's he to get at. So when some walking meat don't give you what he's owin', what he nicked from you in the first place, you takes him to the butcher 'n skin him. That way the next piece've walking meats happy with what's his 'n all. Keep business strait.'

I'm suddenly sorry I accepted the matchstick loan.

As for myself, being in business with the peace herb, violence is an eerie concept. All this talk of flesh and paper skin is, whoh, up there somewhere. Then again, as I have explained, Al's the real criminal. I'm just the victim of inconvenient laws propagated by the bureaucracies of war-mongering, capitalistic imperialists. I even used to tolerate the alcoholic fly that used to come and pollute my rum and coke. Poor darling probably missed me.

'So how'd you do it?'

'Walked up to him, pop, went home.'

'That all?'

'What you expect? The Jackal?'

I suppose not. The Jackal wasn't roasting in a cell with a discredited herbalist.

'Don't work the way them writers put it you know. You's going to do what you's going to do. None of them plots or plans, nor all them emotional things. You've got to do it, you do it, it's over. That's all.'

'Then you get banged up for a few years?' I volunteer.

He snarls. I guess that comment hit a sporadic neuron somewhere.

'Okay, okay, calm down. Why'd you have to, uhm, skin him?'

'Jimmy said he'd been creaming me. Gave me a touch, Jimmy did, stock at a real low price. Silly dangler went to a new wholesaler. Jimmy don't like being undersold, he's give'n good prices. I don't like being creamed, my boys gotto see I don't take that. So I tells Jimmy I'll do him a favour.'

Have you ever stood in a bell tower at a minute to the hour? 'This Jimmy, he Jimmy the scar?'

'Jimmy the what?' he looks up. Is that humour in his eyes? I guess such things only sound cool when your business card reads, 'Mafia assoc.'.

'Jimmy Constanza. He has a scar, left nostril.'

'Yea, his girl ripped out his nose-ring with her teeth.'

The bell starts ringing, using my brain as the gong. 'You got your *stock* from Jimmy?'

'Yea, why?'

'And the skinless guy with the peephole through his head was liquidated for this, uhm, stock?'

'Listen mate. Weed's big money. What's with you anyhow?'

I gulp my humble whisper, 'I was the weed man, just like spreading all over the place.'

'Huh?'

My head shakes with the sadness of the forcibly de-stoned, 'We're just scum man.'

Al's eyes sink and bulge at the same time. That's not really supposed to be possible, but I've explained about science, prison and panic.

'You keep saying stupid things,' he revs, throwing down his cards, "n you might just be cute tonight.'

Have I mentioned panic?

I better check the tickets in Freud and Socrates; I think they're overdue. Maybe I'm overreacting, but it is not every day you find out you are a killer by proxy.

● ● ●

Yea, I know what you want to ask. Who won the game?

Let's just say after he calmed down and turned his cards to reveal four aces, I smiled and carefully hid the four aces in mine.

Peace man, peace.

Innocent as Sin © W. Maree 2000

The conviction and imprisonment of **Ruth Wyner** for five years and John Brock for four years for allowing the premises of Wintercomfort for the Homeless, a Cambridge charity, to be used for the supply of drugs caused a furore within and without the criminal justice system in December 1999. There were calls for the Prime Minister to recommend pardons and demands for a change in the law, besides sharp criticism of the police who pursued the case and the judge who sentenced the pair, neither of whom had previous convictions. After six months in prison, Ruth Wyner and John Brock were granted bail pending appeal—but before that Ruth sent to *Prison Writing* this account of her feelings and experiences during the early stages of imprisonment.

The Festive Season in Prison

Ruth Wyner

The festive season in prison is a far from happy occasion. A generally depressed atmosphere prevails. Inmates miss their loved ones acutely and, because prison officers want to be with their own family and friends, we are 'banged up' for longer, and more often, and activities are reduced.

I arrived at Highpoint prison in Suffolk the day before Christmas Eve feeling half-demented. I had spent the first night of my incarceration in the police cells at Cambridge: light on continuously, no clean clothes, nowhere to wash, just a bench to lie on and a toilet to piss in.

For the next five days I was at HMP Holloway, where the cells are piled five storeys high with four women in most of them, and they contain a degradation previously beyond my imagination. In my short time there I experienced two cells and eight cell-mates: a drug addict with a ghastly and abusive past, drug importers from Jamaica and the US, an armed robber, someone who stabbed her violent boyfriend, a woman obviously mentally ill and others, offences unknown.

De-bunked at Highpoint jail, my head is pounding from the stress I've left behind—and from the hugely uncomfortable two-hour ride in the aptly named sweatbox, packed into a locked cubicle with a hard plastic seat, coated window, barely room to move and no seatbelt. The Group 4 guard passes a lighter through the gap at the bottom of the door so fags can be lit—the only comfort, even for me, a non-smoker for ten years.

Highpoint is initially a more welcoming environment than Holloway. At reception a prison officer calls me by my first name, though that doesn't last. We are strip-searched and see the nurse, who informs me that my blood pressure is up—something that has never happened to me before.

The other inmates tell me off for referring to the rooms as cells. While there are bars at the windows, we have our own door keys. Barred gates stop us from going further than we are meant to. My room-mate is a noisy but good-natured black Londoner, aged 24. She's a year older than my son. Blacks make up around 50 per cent of the prison population I've met, so far.

As we are late in, there is no time for our belongings to be checked. We are each given a nightdress and a few toiletries before being taken to the unit. The beds are barely less hard than at Holloway. The next morning, Christmas Eve, we start to become acquainted with the many routines.

Highpoint has three units for women, housing more than 200. I'm not allowed to describe the prison layout, for security reasons—though presumably I would be free to do so on my release. Suffice to say that we are surrounded by high fences and barbed wire and gates that have to be continually unlocked and locked, all reminders of our lack of freedom.

I work out the 'best' place to escape and the equipment we would need. All complete fantasy, of course, but the urge to get out is urgent and primitive.

At least there is the chance of an occasional breath of fresh air—and the opportunity to commune with the crows, some of them as big as ducks. They must do well from the detritus of this place, and their ability to fly the fences has a special poignancy.

We are normally banged up for thirteen-and-a-half hours a day, longer at weekends and on Bank Holidays. In between we are allocated pretty menial work or 'education' that is extremely basic, and we can use the gym at allotted times. This is all curtailed over Christmas and New Year.

At other times we can go to the TV room, do laundry and make phone calls using only prison phonecards bought with our limited weekly spend. The cards are used up fast, and we cannot have incoming calls. BT must be making a fortune out of us convicts.

We are a motley crew, sometimes referred to by prison staff as 'girls', which I take as an insult. It infantilises us, all grown women. But I guess it represents the truth of our situation.

For me a maddening feature of prison is the constant noise: pop music blaring out, shouting and banging—often, I suppose, to shut out the pain of being in jail.

I have not been threatened in any way in here. In fact, some of the inmates look out for me. 'You look after us on the outside,' said one, 'so we can look after you in here.'

When you can get to the gym, it's a great way to relieve tension: rowing, cycling and jogging machines, weights and other paraphernalia.

Volleyball is a favourite, also soft tennis and badminton. But over the festive season sessions are cancelled for no given reason—on a whim, it would seem.

The education is so basic that all I am offered is art. I'll probably supplement it with a bit of gardening. I refuse to mop floors. I have not been allowed to have a manual portable typewriter, and I'm appealing against the decision to the Governor No 1.

As a concession to Christmas, there were a few bedraggled bits of tinsel downstairs on the unit. I had to resist urges to rip them down. And there was a Christmas quiz. Two officers managed to make it quite a cheery occasion. We organized ourselves into teams of four. The winners got a pouch of tobacco and the losers had to eat a six-pack of mince pies there and then, leading to much hilarity.

Christmas breakfast was a treat: bacon, egg and sausage with a tomato or baked beans. We ate it from our personally allocated plastic plate, bowl and cutlery. But lunch was a failure: slices of what looked like reconstituted turkey that were stone cold, rock solid bread and Yorkshire puddings and undercooked roast potatoes. The Christmas pudding was tough as leather. I did my best to chew a few mouthfuls from the middle of my slice.

In the evening we were banged up early because of staff shortages, and got sandwiches, crisps and an apple to eat in our rooms for supper.

I went to the Church of England service in the chapel the next day— to get off the unit and to enjoy a few carols. We sang lustily, getting the heaviness off our chests. One woman sang a solo, the beauty of it cutting me to the quick in this harsh environment.

The Bishop of Dunwich was there and tried to pep us up. Other people came too, presumably from local churches. Very kind of them but I felt they were voyeurs of our misery. One woman brought two small children, the sight of whom served only to upset me further. At the end of the service, the minister gave out bars of Toblerone. I found it humiliating but took one anyway, knowing it would give me some comfort.

During the rest of the Christmas break, the skeleton service for inmates continued. After the Bank Holidays some mail came in. I got lots of letters and greetings cards after the event, but that doesn't matter in here. I stuck them on my notice board in true prison fashion—with toothpaste.

I can see the photos of my family from my bed. They look frozen in time. I devour the images, and hope they are managing OK.

On New Year's Eve I woke up feeling low. I'd had another string of dreams where I am excluded from things, left out; I don't count or matter. I showered, got milk from the office for breakfast, which we eat in our rooms, and went down at 9 a.m. to wait for gym. At 9.20 a.m. I heard that it had been cancelled.

Disconsolate, I returned to my room and stared into space for half an hour, then tried to do some yoga but my room-mate kept coming in and out. This was no good. I made myself my treat: a cup of camomile tea with hot water from the urn. Then I read a bit from a large book of Irish fiction, a prison present from a friend, and the concentration brought me back to myself a little. At 11.30 a.m. it was time for lunch, the main meal of the day.

In the afternoon there was to have been a Miss Millennium contest. Several of the women had worked on their costumes. It was cancelled at the last minute, no reason given.

The evening medication had to be collected in the morning—If you didn't know, tough. Various people missed out.

A prison officer wrote a jokey message on the board, about how she and a mate were taking a male colleague out that night for an 'initiation'. Very funny, it might be, if I wasn't banged up in here, unable to celebrate.

By lunch-time bang-up I still felt low, lay on the bed, read and napped, feeling completely unmotivated. When we were opened up I caught a message on the notice board that I had a visit: the family!

So I was sent through the various gates in the various fences and let into the visiting room, after being frisked, searched, divested of my watch and having my pockets emptied.

There they were, waiting: my husband, son and daughter, looking so good. We kissed and hugged (allowed only at the start and end of visits) and settle in to an hour-and-a-half of chat, with much hand-holding, trying to catch up on each other.

I was relieved to hear that they coped well over Christmas, the first one my husband and I have not spent together in 25 years of marriage, and they seemed in pretty good spirits. I guess I did too. Did we put on a good show for each other?

The time went fast. At the end they had to leave first, while I waited to be searched and frisked again. This is the time when loneliness and loss are felt most acutely: those three chairs looked very empty indeed.

Back in the unit, try as I might to stay afloat, I started to sink again. After a desultory tea I watched a bit of TV, millennium celebrations around the country. I could not stand it.

So I reminded myself that the intention of putting me in jail was to punish me, hurt me, cause damage even. I needed to be more self-protective but didn't know how. I made a cup of tea, passing women getting in last-minute phone calls before being banged up. 'You will be sure to see them everyday,' said one as I passed.

We were locked in early again. Everyone seemed a bit agitated, a bit depressed. As it got close to midnight we gathered on the landings, squeezed together, surrounded by restriction, by the gates of thick white bars—two sets behind me, three in front—familiar faces behind them all.

Someone had Radio 1 on loud. Then came the countdown: 5, 4, 3, 2, 1. And we all erupted—yelling, whistling, shouting, hugging, kissing: scenes being repeated throughout the country at this moment.

A large woman smashed a cake tin against the wall, the noise reverberating. Then I was up on a chair, arms high, whoopin' and groovin' with all the rest. 'She's moshin'!' gasped a young black girl, astonished. Too right I was.

But 15 minutes later things had died down, and I was back in my room like most of the others, thinking of those on the outside and straining to pick up their thoughts on the ether.

On New Year's Day we heard we had a good report for our behaviour. But all was not well on one of the other units. I am not allowed to report what happened. They were of course out of order, and people on my unit were quick to condemn the perpetrators. I feel that their actions were surely brought about by extremes of emotion. A senior officer was quick to refute this, saying the people involved were 'only in prison because they want to be'. Extraordinary. All the inmates I have met are desperate to get out.

I just hope I don't get too institutionalised to this life, where there is no responsibility apart from doing as you are told. No need to cook, clean (just a flick round the room), shop, organize your life, care for the family, use your abilities for the benefit of all.

I feel out of sight and out of mind, with virtually no rights, individuality wiped out, feelings, hopes, wishes, my very soul of no import.

'Women's prisons are very different to men's,' said the officer at our brief induction. 'What, you mean women are more emotional?' he was asked. This was just what he did mean. 'I don't want to be cutting you down,' he said, encouraging us to talk about our problems rather than do ourselves in.

I'll save him the heartache. But it is hard to talk openly to one's jailers, who we believe write daily notes on us.

Convicts, jailbirds . . . we are, to use the government's terminology, the most socially excluded of all. This is presumably what they think we deserve, that it's a good job too, while they apparently spend more on incarcerating us than it costs to educate a boy at Eton; while they build more prisons to bang up more and more of us 'girls'.

Turning 50 in Jail

I turn 50 this weekend, celebrating in circumstances vastly different from those of birthdays past. I'm in jail.

This should depress me, that I won't be able to party with friends or get any presents. But it doesn't. I've now done more than three months of my five-year sentence. My appeal is due in around six months, but I have my sights on my parole date, June 2002. Three months doesn't sound long in that context, but prison has already lost its sting—an interesting process. My experience of it is reflected in that of my fellow inmates.

The first two weeks are the worst: you're in shock, traumatised. Depression, acute anxiety and tears come easier than sleep. The cell bang-ups, the power of the prison officers, the loss of personal decision-making are all a deep anguish. You yearn for contact with family and friends, to get outside, to get peace and quiet. Every aspect of prison life feels like an abuse, an assault on your person, the feeling of powerlessness falling into despair.

Over the next few months you adapt, learn the ropes, develop camaraderie with other inmates. The prison officers, after making sure you know who's boss, ease up a bit.

The food is rarely appetising, so bits of fresh fruit, a little pepper to transform a tomato, or an onion picked from the gardens to spice up a plain sandwich all become as good as a feast.

After three months I feel steady, know I can cope, have begun to cruise, my fear of prison dissipated, despite inevitable times of depression.

Of course prison is damaging. It's easier to cope with it if you can maximise your laziness. You learn to be devious to get what you want, but you lose the skill of making your own decisions and of being responsible for yourself. Health suffers from the poor food and lack of fresh air: Here at Highpoint you don't get the hour of daily exercise set out in Prison Service rules. This and some other prisons can't figure out how to fit it in with their staffing and the daily routine.

I've taken up smoking again after ten years. Practically everyone smokes, spurred on by boredom and lack of comforts, and some use illegal drugs. I try to limit the damage of smoking by having hearty sessions in the gym.

Since punishment is the main apparent aim of prison—fulfilling society's perceived need for retribution—an inmate cannot escape being damaged. Though the pain of the first few weeks dissipates, it doesn't go away but is buried, but the stress emerges in different ways. I get quite a few headaches. Some people act out their anger and despair by behaving badly or noisily, or harming themselves. You coarsen, harden up. Everyone enjoys relief in getting one over on the screws.

A lot of inmates are already hurt by difficult, disrupted lives and become further alienated by their incarceration. Life is very unfair.

Rehabilitation seems to be a secondary consideration. Prison 'education' has changed in the past few years. Creativity is no longer encouraged and classes rarely offer opportunities for it.

Available at Highpoint are all-round Key Skills and NVQs at the lowest levels. Work is basic: cleaning, kitchen work, gardening (my choice; it's good to get outside, though much of it is heavy labour), sewing and general skivvying here and there. The art class is the loosest one. I bemoan my lack of ability. I find self-expression through words, but I'm not yet allowed a typewriter or access to word processing.

Those jailed for drug offences are sent on drugs awareness courses, though inmates seem pretty drugs aware to me.

There's a unit run as a community, good for trying to overcome some of the alienation, but in my view it's hampered by having a strong Christian focus. This has the potential for causing further alienation and I'm not quite sure how it squares with the prison's equal opportunities policy. A unit for drug rehabilitation is to be set up this year, professionally run, and will no doubt be an asset.

I'm an old bird doing bird. Practically all the others are younger. Many are around the age of my eldest child, in their mid-20s. I don't see the real point of incarcerating most of them for months or years. Unless they are a danger to society, it seems entirely negative.

Damage to the individual damages the whole. Rehabilitation is far better effected in the community.

Meanwhile, the prison officers know all too well that prison loses its bite after the first few weeks. Some of them tell me they wonder how they could package that early experience, keep it going to provide the ultimate deterrent. I protest, saying that would be cruel.

But there's a frightening seriousness in their statements. They know they're not being effective in the work they do, seeing people come back time and again.

I wonder if the Home Office will ever see much past the bang 'em up mentality. More and more of us are getting imprisoned with longer sentences, and especially more women. This, despite the gruelling effect on families who, as the saying goes in here, 'do your sentence with you'. Yet more damage. We know it doesn't make sense.

Prisoners are out of sight and out of mind but play an important role, taking the badness out of society and out of the ordinary law abiding citizen, if there is such a thing. We are the hook to hang it on.

Until the reality of this dynamic is acknowledged nothing will change. In fact, as the prison population continues to increase things will only get worse.

The Festive Season in Prison © Ruth Wyner 2000

Mark Read was born in Sandhurst, England in 1962. His family moved to Seattle when he was four years old. A fascination with trains and hobos led him to abandon a normal life in his teens, to travel the rails to California. Returning to Seattle he became addicted to heroin, which led to homelessness and petty crime. He was eventually sentenced to 109 months for a series of robberies.

A story by Mark Read, 'Ticket to Torment', was published in *Prison Writing* No. 9 while he was in Florence Correctional Institution, Colorado. In February 1999 he was released from Louisiana Federal Detention Center and deported back to England, despite having lived almost all his life in the USA. He now lives in Romsey, Hampshire.

A book of Mark Read's prison poems and drawings, *Steel Bars and Dirty Concrete* was published in 1997. This story, 'Mellaril' exemplifies Mark Read's style and subject matter—the desperate isolation and oppression of what prisoners call America's Gulag

Mellaril

Mark Read

You sit on the bare concrete floor, in a tiny windowless holding cell on the first floor of the prison's hospital, stewing in the nothingness of waiting. Waiting. Seems like you are always waiting on something or someone. But you have the forbearance of a rock. Do not care. You have been transformed into a non-person. Waiting.

Two hours? Three hours? You jump inside yourself every time you hear the whisper of feet on the other side of the door. Your knocks and pleadings, unanswered. For you are a cog that will not fit in anybody's wheel, especially the iron-strong cog of rehabilitation.

Under direct fluorescent lighting the cell's emptiness presses its weight of years, the years of silence. A silence that bespeaks eternity and all final things. It goes deep, opens you up, and then takes you down into its depth where you can see something in front of you—your door, your gate, your death, the pure terrain of time. The air grows defunct and you feel like you are being smothered. You break out in a cold sweat and your heart pounds fearfully. All reality is a naked question.

To eradicate your claustrophobia, you begin pacing; each step and exercise of some anxiety not provided by instinct. Twelve steps one way, twelve steps the other. Rubber sandals sighing against concrete.

While you pace, you explore the sadly green walls that you associate with time and death. You take in every imperfection, read every carving, while trying hard not to perceive the glassy streaks of hardened snot. That only clarifies your dire position.

What am I? Why am I here? What must I do?

Your hopeless sense of abandonment, combined with the actuality of what you have been reduced to—an eight digit number—overpowers your despair and depression, fuelling you into a fit of rage. You take out your anger on the steel door with a driving force. Every kick exploding through the building, shattering the unearthly silence, as gathering impulse of your devoid civilization, target your mind, pushing the density of your thoughts into a vital white heat that erupts from your throat.

You smile to your knowing as hurried footsteps and jingling keys abound the hallway, stopping in front of the cell. The cardboard covering the cell door's window is swiftly removed. A pale, hard-looking face with orange beard stubble looks in. Keys rattle, the lock disengages, and the door slowly opens—cautiously.

'What in the hell's the matter, Readtino?'

You look up at the guard, almost apologetically, and find yourself staring into the most cankerous pair of eyes you have ever discerned: bloodshot, turbid, and so full of hate, you break your gaze and, instead, make a focal point on the pathetic lump of flesh that is his nose, which is splayed and puffy and has the texture of bleached asphalt, fissured and cracked.

'You on drugs, boy? What in the hell's your problem? You keep kickin' on the goddamn door, I'm gonna writcha up!'

'I need to get out of this cell . . . feeling—feeling something really bad. Really bad!' And not able to look the guard in the face, you stare down at your hard-rubber sandals and protruding white toes. Toes appearing freakish.

'Well ya ain't goin' nowhere till the doc sees ya, so . . . sit down and quit makin' a rackit!'

You glare at the guard for what he is—a mindless box of rocks who looks but one step short of Down's syndrome, sigh hugely, and howl a banshee moan. Asphalt face slams the door, locks it, and immediately begins babbling into his two-way radio.

'Code seven, hospital, code seven, hospital.'

Safe on the other side of the door, the guard gawks at you through the tiny window, mocking you with an idiot smile, revealing his true self: man that didn't add up in the mathematics of life, and whose guiding principles flowed from a centre of persecution. You are unable to control the gravitation pull of madness, and you lash back at the door. Asphalt Face laughs—a forced laugh.

Your heart thrashes as heavy footsteps and a crush of voices flood the hallway. And while the newcomers—one-by-one—peer in at you sizing up the situation, Asphalt Face fills them in.

'Mr. Readtino,' says a dough-boy looking face with big ears and a spray of old acne scars. 'I'm Lieutenant Moran . . . Now just what seems to be the problem?'

You laugh insanely, and then spit on the window.

For time—standing minutes—there is only murmured conversation and the crowded squelch of two way radios. The huddle before the strike. You can sense the inevitable in contracting bowels, the punishment to come.

Retreating to the far end of the cell, you climb onto the combination toilet/sink, and position yourself. Seconds later, the door clicks free and in rush a gang of goons. Dressed for a small war. they sport padded vests and rubber truncheons, with full-face helmets that resemble something out of a 'B' Hollywood space flick. And leading this band of oppressed bozos, wielding a canister of pepper mace, is Asphalt Face himself.

'Mr.Readtino . . . I need ya to step down from the commode, then kneel on the floor with your forehead against the wall, placing you hands behind your back!'

You laugh. You cannot see Asphalt Face's mouth, which is concealed behind his respirator, but you can tell by his loony large eyes that he's grinning.

'If you refuse to do as I ordered, Mr. Readtino . . . '

You leap from the toilet and half-catch Asphalt Face by his respirator, knocking the both of you to the floor, where under a hail of rubber truncheons you are beat of all resistance. You lay limp as the merry crew of degenerates secures you in cuffs and shackles.

'How's it feel, tough guy?' jeers Asphalt Face. And when you do not reply—cannot reply, he maces you directly in the face. You feel as if a flame is consuming you from the inside out, extinguishing all fight.

'Take 'im to the third-floor and four-point 'im!'

Transporting you is a group affair: one guard on each leg and arm, while one of the guards who has you by arm drives your head forward using your ponytail as a handle. You berate yourself for having grown your hair three-years long.

Suddenly, without warning, you are dropped to the floor, cracking your forehead. A booted foot keeps you in place. You know you are in an elevator by the way the floor swayed when you were dropped to the floor, and the distant emanations that only elevators seem to contain: dust, and machinery that's been worked hard.

Whosh—the third floor.

You are dragged, pulled, and half-carried into a cell, where you are forcefully positioned on a plastic-covered mattress. You lay docile, eyes closed, while you are briskly secured four-point: Both ankles and wrists fastened to iron rungs with shackle cuffs. And once secured, a heavy-handed guard, using a pair of scissors, cuts off all of your clothing but for your underwear.

Footsteps retreat. Keys jangle and doors close. You are alone in a strained silence.

Slowly, ever so slowly, you force your eyes open and hold them so, fighting the problem burning which eventually subsides. When your vision swims back into focus, you are met with a point of light that could be described as neither daylight nor dusk, as it pours in through the cell's caged window, it's metrical alive. You take in your new surroundings.

The cell held a veteran sadness and is unlike any other cell you've been housed in. Walls rise powerfully, coldly, painted in a placating pink. In the right-front corner of the cell, where the wall curves for what would normally hold plumbing, there is only a grate mounted in the cement floor. The raw stench of sewage connecting with this discovery. And beyond the facade of inch-thick iron bars, there's a tiny freehold and then an oversized wooden door with a triangular formed door. Clumps of dried toilet paper and mouldy food pepper the door, walls and ceiling that you intuit as forgotten remnants of a forgotten protest.

Minutes to hours . . . Your attention is lured to voices and the distinguishable squeak of an oil-less wheel, soon followed by the wavering odor of prisonhouse fare, running up under the door.

'What about 303?' says a female voice, followed by a ghost of a face peering in at you through the window.

You smile in acknowledgement. 'He's in restraints!'
Murmured conversation, and then the door opens admitting a starchy-faced woman, her blue-gray hair wound up in a beehive. Opening the second door of bars, she enters the cell.

'You gonna be good if I get you out of them restraints?' she asks, her face full of question, thickened with concentration. You nod your head for yes. 'Let me finish handin' out the rest of these dinner trays, and then I'll be right back. Promise!'

The benevolence of her manners leaves you awashed in confusion, generating such a rush of emotions that scratch deep at memory and haven't been used in years—you feel that there might be hope for a future yet.

And as good as her word the nurse returns shortly, carrying a food-tray, her presence the color of life, splashing you with her every word. She lets herself in and, removing a sizeable ring of brass keys from her smock pocket, unfetters you. Not a hint of trepidation in her disposition.

'Meatloaf with choc'late cake for dessert,' she says; and then removing the lid from the dinner tray, she places the tray on the end of the bed. 'Doctor Howland should be by in a while, so—enjoy your dinner and relax, and hopefully sometime later, we'll be able to get you moved into one of the regular cells.'

You search your small bag of words for something to say, wanting to express your swelling gratitude for her kindness, but before you are able to find the appropriate words, she leaves.

Drawn to the dinner tray, you stare at the slab of meatloaf until it changes shape. Seven years in the joint and you've never so much as tasted this looming dish—and you're not about to start now. Nothing but the roll and cake have a chance.

Dinner over, you begin pacing the cell; the mathematics of counting corners, bars, cracks in the floor occupying your mind. You pace until the hard-rubber sandals generate a crop of blisters, compelling you to lie down on the bare, plastic mattress.

From your prone position, the cell seems exceptionally huge, silent. You feel removed, severed, alien to the earth's plain. You dwell on the thought of how many other poor motherfuckers had lain in this exact position, and whom like yourself, had met a destructive onslaught of redneck justice.

Subconsciously, your hand has slipped beneath the waistband of your underwear—scratching, probing, searching out the pea-sized lump you had recently discovered in your left teste, and you are suddenly cognizant of your erect member; and so kicking off your underwear and positioning yourself, you begin masturbating, frantically.

You are so deep in the undertow of self-inflicted ecstasy, you don't even hear the outer wooden door as it opens.

'Oh!' says the nurse, startled, startling you.

You sit up so rapidly, it's as if every drop of blood in your body has gushed to your head at once, leaving you reeling. Your cheeks and scalp burn with the heat of shame. Awkwardly, you reach for your underwear and slip into them.

'Don't look so guilty,' says the nurse as she opens the second door of bars. 'I've worked here long enough to've made my fair-share of poorly-timed entrances.'

You look up into the nurse's face, wanting to reply, to say something, anything, but cannot.

'Boy, ya sure didn't eat much, did ya now . . . Though I don't blame ya one bit. Meatloaf was never one of my fav'rite meals.' And as she bends to gather the dinner tray, she drowns you with a buttery smile—a smile that makes you feel backwards, childishly slow. You say, though more out of discomposure then inquisition, 'Do you think I'll be moved to one of the regular cells soon?'

'Well that's up to Doctor Howland, and he . . . '

'Did I hear . . . doctor?' says the gaunt-faced new-comer, who presses by the nurse and enters the cell. And as if on cue, the nurse makes a quick departure.

The receptive Doctor Howland, tall, thin, worldly and ethereal, his nametag pinned upside-down above his left breast, lowers himself to the floor, half-lotus, and then stretching his face into a smug—but shooting—grin, offers you a hand.

'So Mark,' says the doctor as he opens your medical file. 'Just what seems to be the problem?'

'Problem?' you stutter.

'Yes. From what Dr.Tubb tells me you have quite a past history of self-mutilation, hearing voices, and paranoid delusions. But if I'm correct, this had been while you were incarcerated in the state system,' says the doctor, who then looks at you with delving eyes, as if you are supposed to confirm this. But you say nothing, your mental faculty void. And as the doctor looks back into your file, he says, 'Have you ever been psychologically treated while in the federal prison system?' You nod your head for no. 'That's interesting,' says the doctor, who is now studying your face so earnestly it's as if he's looking for some hidden message that would resolve everything.

'I do understand that you're a little upset over what happened this afternoon, Mark, but if you don't put up a little effort and begin communicating with me, and let me know what's going on up here . . . ' pointing to his head 'I'm afraid it might be some time until you're returned to population.' And as you endure the doctor's gaze—a gaze that seems to contain two forms of life, the subject matter and its hidden implications—you say, 'I don't really know. It's just that ... sometimes my thoughts are too much to comprehend, and the only way I can seek relief is through ... pain!'

'How long have you been experiencing these type of thoughts?' demands the doctor, his fingers configurating into a steeple.

'Years. Ever since I crossed that time-barrier when my dreams and hopes were replaced with reality, and I was able to discern the great complexities of life in the reflection of my fragile existence. Why I...'

'The voices, Mark. What exactly do the voices tell you? Do they tell you to hurt yourself?'

Diverting your attention, you are drawn to a tiny cockroach as it effortlessly works its way up and over one of the doctor's shoes—soft shoes, sensible shoes—and begins climbing a pant leg.

'Mr Readtino,' says the doctor, trilling the 'T' in your last name, his tone of voice rash. And your reply, you say, 'It would be too hard to explain . . . I don't know—no, in fact I know—there are not words in which I can express what I sometimes hear.'

Silence. The doctor's steeple of fingers expands into palms, as if he's expressing your lack of willingness to communicate.

'Well I'm short for time right now, Mark, but I'd like to get together with you sometime tomorrow, probably in the morning, to continue our discussion.' And then pulling himself up with the help of the bars, his face stretched into a self-satisfied grin as if he was reflecting some heavy calculation, he bends and dusts off his powder-blue corduroy pants, knocking off the cockroach, which he unknowingly steps on as he works the feeling back into a sleepy leg.

Then looking at his watch, and then at you, he says, 'I'll see about getting you moved into a proper cell, and, sometime later this evening—I think it's around nine when they hand out meals—there'll be something to help you sleep and keep everything up here . . . ' pointing to his head 'in good working order.'

'Something . . . for me?' you say.

'Yes. Have you ever been on any psychotropic medications?' You nod your head for yes. 'Have you ever taken Mellaril?' You nod your head for no. 'Well then I think I'll start you on a low dose of Mellaril, and we'll see if it doesn't help you. But remember, Mark, in order for you to benefit from a drug such as Mellaril, it's important that you take it consistently. See you tomorrow, Mark.'

And as you watch the doctor close and lock the barred door, you are plunged into a pool of silent regret. For you had wanted to convey the awesomeness of your condition, but, there was only that keying you have come to live with, a keying symphony of dark withdrawal.

Once again you begin pacing; 12 steps one way, 12 steps the other.

Mellaril © Mark Read 2000. Mark Read's book of poems and illustrations, *Steel Bars and Dirty Concrete*, is available in the USA from Oakfield Publishers, Seattle, price $8.95. United Kingdom readers who wish to purchase a copy can be put in contact with the author via *Prison Writing*.

Imprisoned in England after spending eleven and a half years in South African prisons, **S. D. Hewett** found big differences in the two systems— some good and some bad. Here, he compares education, food and visits, among other things, and draws a conclusion as to which system is most effective in helping prisoners towards release.

Pros and Cons

S. D. Hewett

If you have ever been unfortunate enough to be a guest of one of Her Majesty's prison's, you will, one time or another, have walked around in the exercise yard. Whether in Albany, or Whitemoor the conversations one hears on the yard are almost always the same; in a few instances the tone, language or level of enthusiasm might change, but never the subject matter.

While walking around the yard, snippets of conversations from different cliques always leave me thinking that (a) many prisoners don't know how lucky they are and (b) they seem to have got the wrong end of the stick. Comments such as 'The food tasted like crap again today', 'Bloody three weeks I've been waiting for a book on order from the outside library', 'They keep on showing us the same videos over and over', 'Why is it that I have to ask for a grant to pay for my studies?', 'The police or my brief stitched me up', and on and on it goes along these lines. I must confess that just lately I've been falling into this way of thinking, but having had experience of the prison system in another country I keep my mouth closed and think to myself that we seem to have got our priorities wrong. It is not the food, library or education that are the problems in the British prison system. What *is* important is our attitudes towards one another and staff, the time we are out of cell and the types of activities available to us in the form of hobbies etc. while we are behind the door, as well as some form of meaningful employment.

In Britain, when arrested you are entitled to a solicitor free of charge and your interviews with the police are recorded. The food provided is usually the type of TV dinner that is bought in Tesco or Safeways. You will not be kept in custody indefinitely and if later convicted of a crime, any time you spend in custody will be deducted from your sentence.

South Africa, where I have also been in prison, does not provide such conditions that we all here take for granted. If you cannot afford a solicitor then you will not have one unless it is a capital offence and then you will only be told of this once the police have finished *interviewing* you which can take up to three weeks. The food is not worth mentioning and oh, did I forget to say that *the interviews* are not recorded and the means used to extract information would not seem out of place in China or Iraq? Forget about any time spent in custody or remand being taken off your sentence, you're dreaming.

Ah, the Land of Hope and Glory! In British prisons we are given the choice of different food at mealtimes, education is free, cells are heated, we receive a basic wage—not much, admittedly—every week even if not employed, access to a library, free newspapers and most important an Ombudsman, who we can write to if we feel that we have been treated unfairly. All this and much more are what we take for granted and often complain about.

The number of organizations and charities existing in Britain to help prisoners and their families is quite astonishing. In South Africa only one comes to mind—the Probation Service. The importance and promotion of education in British prisons can be seen in the wide range of courses available from the Three R's right through to Open University degrees. There is access to materials, teachers and computer facilities that plenty of people on the outside would envy.

I am a good example of the differences in the two countries' attitudes towards education. All I had to show for having spent eleven and half years in the South African prison system was a sharp, sly, cunning mind. One that had only contempt for the weak and saw them as natural prey. All I took with me on the day I walked out of the gates was hate and loathing for the system and all in it. I also had the reputation of being a good smuggler and membership of the most violent and ruthless gang inside and out of the prison system. Yet, in the few years that I have been inside the British prison system, not only has my use of the English language improved to such an extent that I now consider myself just as fluent as in my first, which is Afrikaans.

This has been achieved through GCSEs in English Language and Literature. I have also had the opportunity to complete GCSEs in Dutch, while studying for my Maths GCSE—and I've not let the world of technology get away from me as I have completed numerous certificates and diplomas in computer and business technology. I would not have been able to achieve these in a South African prison.

The only education you might get for free in South Africa, if you are totally illiterate, are the Three R's. Anything more than that you will have to organise and fund yourself. Tutors, time off from work and facilities for anything other than the Three R's are just not there, although you might get some time off just before the exams to study in cell. When it comes to gainful employment it's a totally different story. The different types of trades available from bricklayer, carpenter, electrician, plumber, motor mechanics and so on are taken very seriously and you can do a four to five year apprenticeship which will lead to a trade test to become a qualified tradesman. This is one of the few advantages South African prisons have over Britain.

Like Britain, all South African prisons have a library, but that is as far as the likeness goes. Whereas here we are given access at least once a week and are able to order books from the outside library services if not available in the prison library, in South Africa I was lucky to get to a library once every fortnight even in the best of prisons. The content of books available were not in the slightest way educational or recreational. If you were a western bluff or interested in the history of the 'Boer' then you were in your element, but if you wanted to read about the other people of South Africa e.g. the Xhosa or Zulu you had no chance. The thought of being able to order a book through the library from outside was ludicrous.

Now food: here, jacket potatoes, chips, saute potatoes, mashed potato, roast potato and boiled potatoes are just the few different types of potato dishes on the menu, as well as vegetables and all the options of other dishes such as pork chops, liver, pies, burgers, gammon, Yorkshire pudding, pasties, chicken, salads and much, much more . . . We haven't even come to the sweet or the continental and cooked breakfast yet. I can't try to begin to explain the type of breakfast in a South African prison, but the best was the once a week bowl of oats. Well, it was until I saw the sacks it came in, with the words 'Not fit for human consumption' stencilled on them. They were, and probably still are, feeding them horse feed.

Lunch in South African prisons is the only cooked meal of the day. Notice I didn't say hot. The only variety of the vegetables is that if you had raw carrots and boiled cabbage yesterday you most properly will get boiled carrots and raw cabbage today. Meat, as in pork and lamb chops, you will be lucky to have twice a year at Christmas and New Year, otherwise the normal menu consists of 'chicken a la dynamite', bones and insides included. The only pork you get is boiled blocks that have more fat and hair on them than meat. Brawn pieces (offal) and Soya comes more than one day a week. What passes for rice, I've never seen anything like it since. Sunday was the one day I could look forward to—I got a chicken drumstick for lunch. As for sweet, that falls into the same category as pork and lamb chops.

Suppertime (tea) consists of six slices of brown bread and a bit of jam, cool drink or soup depending on the time of year. A boiled egg or piece of cheese is given with tea on Wednesdays and Sundays. Think of this every time you feel like complaining about the fact you did not get a poppadom with your curry and rice.

Visits in South Africa are conducted with a perspex partition between you and your visitors. Only if you are an A group (enhanced level) are you allowed contact visits, although visits are permitted more often than in Britain.

Visits is the one area where Britain is still in the dark ages. Contact visits in some prisons are conducted in such uncomfortable conditions and atmosphere; chairs that are screwed to the floor and tables which scrape your shins raw are not what I'd call an ideal setting. In South Africa, once you have reached the enhanced level, you will have visits in surroundings that make it easy for you to feel relaxed enough to enjoy the time spent on visits; your family are not looked upon as potential drug smugglers and they are treated with respect at all times. At Christmas and New Year, special provisions are made so that you call have all day visits and your family can bring along snacks to eat; in some prisons you can even have a barbecue.

Here in Britain visits are made out to be so good with the facilities available, but in reality this is all about waiting for the visit to begin, not the visit itself. Christmas and New Year are times when families want to be together the most, but there are no visits at all. Now this *is* something to be pissed off about.

Hobbies and time spent out of cell on association is another area where Britain falls way behind. The type of hobbies you are allowed to have is restricted in such a way due to security reasons that it can be more of a pain than a pleasure to pursue a hobby. Whereas in South Africa they are encouraged to such an extent that you can do almost anything as long as it does not involve using hacksaw blades, here you can't even have certain pens or paints. Though it must be said that creativity is encouraged very much, but that is due to outside organisations—like *Prison Writing*—who have nothing to do with the Prison Service.

'Association' is a word that I used to believe meant a group of people coming together for the purpose of some shared ideal or activity, never did I think it would come to mean the time spent out of cell to watch TV etc. The amount of time we are out of cell and the conditions it is spent in are something I still find hard to come to terms with. It is hard to make a phone call while there are two televisions blaring away, not enough seats for everybody to sit down and the space in which we are kept for association much to small. After having spent five-and-a-half years in prison I'm still a B cat and I'm locked up in my cell on average 18 hours a day. Surely this is an aspect of prison life that should be looked at and worked on?

In South African prisons there is no such thing as association. You are opened up in the morning and, depending on the prison you in, you are open until you get locked up at night. If you are on enhanced level then you will not be locked in your cell at night, you will be locked up only if you are on a lower level. TVs, hotplates and access to the gym are available at all times, as long as you are not skiving off work to do it. Weekends you are left to do your own thing and sports events are organized by the inmates rather than the officers. The time spent in a cell is a bare minimum and is basically left up to you to decide how and what you do with you spare time. You are given the choice.

I am basing all of the above on personal experience. As I left the South African prison system in 1994, some of the things may have changed for the better or worse. But it is plain for me to see that the very things we tend to complain about here are not likely to be improved as they are already at a high level, compared to most. It is the things that we don't talk about, believing that it can't be improved, that need changing. There are pros and cons in every system and having experienced two different systems I know which one I would choose if given a choice. Britain may be far behind in its attitude about prisons and its inmates, but the institutions made available to prisoners through outside agencies such as education, help with addictions, a place to live after release, support for the family of prisoners give the opportunity to improve and better yourself so that you have a greater chance upon release in this country.

When things are not going your way we must not try to shoot down the good things and privileges the system has to offer. Rather, we must make use of it the best we can and try to improve and better ourselves so we have a chance upon release. The things that need improving are what we must look at and try better. What I do know is that it's not the things I hear being complained about on the yard. After all this is not supposed to be a holiday camp.

Pros and Cons © S. D. Hewett 2000

Poems by Cisse Amidou

Cisse Amidou is Nigerian. In 1991 she was sentenced to life imprisonment in Thailand. With the help of Amnesty International, her sentence was reduced to 40 years in 1996. She is presently held in Lardyao Women's Prison in Bangkok where she seeks inspiration through her writing.

The Night of Execution Day

The wind kicked off over night
Its noise whistling mischievously
roaring through the prison barricades
The thunder strikes coherently
Its colour hissing anonymously
maddening anger
Its hidden demeanor is to call
out for the rain.
The prison yard thick with noise
and darkness:
an omen preparing the prisoner
for death.
The cloud rolled past through angry
darkened gray clots. Clenching
its teeth, celestial dust devil
tumbling across a low blue sky.
The prisoner locked the imaginary
mind with imaginary lock
throwing the imaginary key away.
Tiny drops of rain making a
turbulent noise across the roof of
the prison.
The prisoner laying on the bare
humid floor chained to the
wall like a wounded dragon.
Thoughts darkenly belaboured
wishing for the last wish
The wish,
'The wish is to walk around
the city seeing its halogen
crime light staining the
otherwise lively horizon.
The wish
The wish is to marvel in the city's
Malignancy's sickly orange aura
with its vast mostly bubble

of postular gas and the beauty that
spout overnight in a
burst of civic priapism, overburdened
the prisoners turbulent mind'
'Never had thought would come
to the city to be executed.'
The beautiful city with its vibrant
lights ought to be more powerful
than the law of execution.
Aircraft taking off from the aerodrome
nearby roaring through the torrent of rain.
The flooded mind refusing to decide
on which was much offensive—
The disturbance during the night
of the execution or the final
destination and habitation of the cadaver.
'Heaven or hell'
The cold front swollen erupting
through caged holes blasting
with an untamed destruction,
engulfing the prisoner's body.
Pain of death could have
been so sweet rather
than facing executioner's
face and weapon.
The prisoner closes eyes,
the mind savouring in death
by cold wind.
The rattling of keys,
loud whispers of executioners
jilted the prisoner back to
reality. Today is the death day:
'an issuance of an assurance of either heaven or hell.'

Prayer for the Needy

Seven years have passed Angel face
Seven years since I have
loved and touched you,
yet,
You will always be the love
of my life;
seven years my beloved, my dove;
I dwell among the unknown.
Land Beyond ocean and seas.
But: Never I forget your needs in my prayers.
I lay upon my tiny squared bed;

Imagining
Your beautiful eyes;
Your ever resilience being.
On my tiny squared bed;
I know you need me to pray for you.
Seven years, my honey, my love
In one of those sweet dreams
I slept;
I prayed for all your needs:
To love you more and more
Your presence is always with me,
In this strange land.
My beloved daughter:
All the prayers I make
Knowing nature never did betray
the heart that loves.
Through all the years of our lives
I pray for your needs
To strengthen from joy to joy
I pray for moon to shine over thee
In thy straight path.

Death Row

Behind the wall, here no loved ones
lurked around except the voices of
million crickets. Proclaimed I to die
by execution.
What crime commit I o'er decision made?
'Me mingled with white silverish dust'
Though I cannot understand a word
but know I the judge sentenced me to die
The furiness in the eyes of the judge
sentenced me to die by execution
'Me to die 'cause me disrespect dreamy powder'

The Judge Need Not Listen To My Plea

Neither doth care for my innocence,
'better dead than living' sterned voice declared.
He condemned me to live solitarily
before my death day among the dead souls,
hatred hizzing from his buzzling self
as he dug me my grave
Joyful satisfactory red tears dripping down
the corner of his bulging eyes,

as he condemned me to dwell
amongst the condemned living souls
loved ones he forbidden me see;
I plead for some to solicit
Solicitor I'll never have
'cause money failed me have'
Money I cannot have 'cause the judge
has proclaimed me to die by execution.
Condemned soul have no right
Condemned soul has no say
Neither does have last wishes.
Lay I down on the lonely cold floor
Naked gloriously my statues being
using the hair on my body for
protection where no blankets offered.
Manacles dressing my ankles, my only
joy, pride and remembrance of my plight.
Menades make loud noise while I
walk, my inmates vow to kill me
before my death day.
'Me think they crazy to want to stay quiet'.
I walk, manacles chatter last songs of glory
My inmate screamed 'cause they think
I must be crazy to walk and make noise.
'Screams we all make like wounded lions
Came to an halt, we started mourning
Man beside me, called to his death
While I wait my turned envied.
Though I wait for my death day,
I wished dead before my death date.
Blissfully would I have sailed
through peaceful pilgrim
Saints conveying me in a crystal
bucket, where heaven or hell
N'er matter: but my soul will
 have its say, right and
last wish finally.'

Dream

She woke up from her sleep
deep sweet dream
Angels lay her
among the flowers
Roses, Irises and Daffodils
Many colours are they
Countless are they

Red, purple, green, yellow, blue, white
And tiny sprinkled stars;
With rays of glory enveloping
Her beautiful image
In her dream, she was dressed
In white silk and colorful diamonds
All around her beautiful and sparkling
like the star crackers.
Though in her sleep
realization
Vividly it could be a dream
There is a strong will it should be reality
Don't stop beautiful sweet dream
Never you stop.
Stop you are; stop the world.

My Lost Years

Rivulets of tears pouring down my eyes
I bit hard on my lower lips to control it
But just like the uncontrollable dungeon
I am in, it couldn't be controlled.
Rivulets of shame written all over me
Shame of not wanting the next prisoner
Sleeping beside me to know I am crying.
'For tomorrow it could be all around
the prison'. Though we are sharing
the same faith, but never the same souls.
How could I account for all the lost years?
'How can I bear the thoughts of God.,
not listening to my voice, while even
in prison, He does much for other
people?' How could I merge my lost
years with the loss of fulfilment in me?
How could God let the striking hunger
in me combine with the striking
freedom in me.
I bow down everyday to pray.
The hunger accurate with the indefinite.
Time and term of both persist.
Confinement and hunger. I never see
before and I never want to see again.
Never going to have lost years again.

Day-to-Day…

Day-to-Day . . .

George Hayes began writing while in prison. Aged 28 and serving a life sentence in Wakefield, the following is an extract from his as-yet unpublished novel, *Slipping*. A harsh but vivid fictional account of relationships in the darker corners of contemporary society, the author makes the characters and events tell the story in an honest, unsensational style.

Slipping

George Hayes

Chapter 1: Ray of Light of Light

A few hours earlier it had been Friday 15 May, another Big Free and Sexy night. In the back room comfort of his West End club, Raymond Fletcher sat slouched in a large, leather, purple chair. The lights were dimmed and his tree trunk legs were crossed, the heels of his feet were poised on some body building magazine on the edge of the table.

Expressionless, he observed the night's activities through monitors. On the table lay a white ice hockey face mask, the one he had been wearing earlier on the dance floor, to compliment an all black shiny baseball kit.

A little over-indulged with drink, and much more with drugs, he decided to call it a day or night, or whatever it was, and head home. Raymond was never one to relax in the warm glow that followed sex. At times, he was simply bored to death being at the club, even though, in reality, he did not need to be there. He liked to hang around for the 'just in case'.

Raymond Fletcher had made it a long time ago. Now 36 years old, it was eight years since had given up being a bouncer, and he had come a long way since then. His personal philosophy of life had materialised in himself. 'Build the muscles on the body first and then chase your dreams after'. He was a big guy, six-two, 22 and a half stones of dense muscle. Fifteen years of dedicated weight training, and hard anabolic steroid abuse, made his already large frame look as if he could easily be the World's Strongest Man. Now he sold steroids imported from East Europe, plus any other type of drug the client might want.

Breathing silently, he relaxed in the air conditioned coolness, turned it on full blast, to dry up the dampness of exertion only moments earlier on the sofa bed next door.

His office colour scheme was a gaudy purple, black, and yellow combination. The room with the bed was simply black and gold. It showed what he thought of as good taste.

He had a mind that most politicians would envy. Raymond Fletcher would do anything, so long as he was right, for as far as he was concerned, his combination of mental and physical power, elevated him to a status of invincibility. In fact, he was untouchable. So should there be an incident in the early hours of a Saturday morning at his club, not only could Raymond be the first to react, but again he could be proved right.

But tonight had been a good night. No real problems at all; and his security staff had the right reputation to keep it that way. They also controlled all the business, while he, as usual, fucked some bitch that was high on drugs, and swore she was aching for him, who had to have it. In what seemed like a reluctant manner of 'just doing you a favour,' he pounded with no mercy until she became a quivering wreck, and soon after passed out.

The office was designed for many eventualities. The strong point being The Alarm Situation, as Raymond would say—a raid by the police. But now he just sat back in a comfortable chair, and watched the routine club night on flickering screens.

He had some time ago left the fucked girl laying face down on the sofa bed, and phoned his doorman, Warren, to get his car, and 'Bring it round front.' He was getting impatient.

Swinging his feet from the table, he sat forward, sniffed some coke off a mirror. Then he got up and walked over to the fridge that was by the window. He looked out of it through the blinds just from habit, then took out two bottles of Heineken Export, before going to sit back down, restless now.

After finishing the second bottle, he got up, and went to see where the fuck Warren had got to. Leaving the office area, he walked straight into the club's crowded hot atmosphere, not appreciating having to do the journey through the noisy revellers, but soon he was outside, at the front of the club.

'Have you seen Warren?' He asked the two doormen. They told him yeah, but about 20 minutes ago, when he came out.

As if on cue, down the street, a big Merc drifted around the corner, driven by Warren. Ray stroked his funky dreads backwards with his left arm, as if they impaired his vision, although they did not. He jerked his head back and sniffed a couple of times. He could taste the coke, despite the fact that most of his mouth was numb, but not his brain, for he noticed that the car's left wing mirror, (His Merc!), was dangling useless from the side of the door.

And so this was it, his big situation for the night. As Warren stepped out of the car, no matter what he said had happened to the car, Raymond Fletcher was in the position of strength—because he was right. That's how Ray always saw it.

Warren stood facing Raymond through glazed eyes.

'Let me explain,' were his first words, but obviously the wrong choice, because at that point Raymond lay into him. Two punches to the gut in a split second, left-right, and Warren dropped like a dumped sack of potatoes. The first sharp cry of pain from Warren's mouth, was overridden by a second louder one.

Only then did Raymond speak to him, through clenched teeth, as he kicked him along the pavement and onto the road.

Raymond's security men watched, making sure no one left the club to witness the punishment. Not until Ray had got the man bloodied, dazed and crawling on the road, did he order Marvin, the head door attendant, to lift him up, as he opened the boot of his car.

Marvin dropped the helpless Warren in the Mercedes by the tool box. He struggled in vain, and just before the boot shut, Marvin wondered if Raymond was going to kill him.

'Tell Harry to get round my house now!' Raymond screamed to Marvin, his locks swinging out the window, as he turned his head before racing all the way home to Highgate Village.

Marvin slunk back into the club, and made his way to Raymond's office. Once there, he used the phone to call Harry, who was in bed.

If you rang Harry's mobile in the middle of the night, while he was with his woman, you may as well have called the Angel of Death to collect you. Warren was dead already, Marvin thought. He put the receiver down, smiling to himself as he thought about how much he loved his job, working for an individual of principle like Raymond. He looked around the office, and eased back into the purple leather chair.

His eyes focused on a life-sized oil painting that Ray had especially commissioned, of his favourite page three model. It showed her sitting on Raymond's Rolls Royce parked outside his mansion. Wearing only the top half of a leopard-print bikini, she sat on the bonnet of the car, legs astride, feet resting on the bumper. Her naked crutch was teasingly just concealed by the Roll's trade-mark statue standing erect between her thighs. The only part of her that was covered, her breasts, were so phenomenally large, that she might, Marvin thought, as well have been naked. If he asked Raymond about it, he would have got the same lecture on how it showed subtlety, taste, and style. The mansion, the car, the model, the pose, the oils, an unprecedented work of art, it was perfect to him. A modern masterpiece—in its own genre. Yeah Marvin thought, that was what he said, that word genre.

He helped himself to some cocaine that was left idle on the table. Why leave it just laying there? Then he tried on the ice hockey face mask that had been beside the drugs. Mimicking his boss's favourite pose, he crossed his feet, and put them on the table, and sat back, trying to imagine himself as Raymond. 'There you are!' Marvin almost jumped to his feet taking them off the table, as he looked up startled and saw a partly dressed girl emerging sleepily from the room off Raymond's office. She looked about 18, wearing black thigh length leather boots, and a thin pink and blue corset, that Marvin was not going to be fooled by. No, it may have looked like underwear, but he'd seen girls wear dresses like that before, and that was it, the complete outfit. Her hair was untidy, and lipstick smeared all over her cheeks. Umm, he thought, she did look nice, like some X-rated clown.

The girl walked over to the front of the desk, bent over, and sniffed some cocaine. Marvin liked the way she did it, like a veteran.
She spoke again, in a drawling and seductive voice, 'Why did you leave me Ray?'

He was shaken, and at a loss for words, so he just removed the mask, bracing himself for when she realised that he was not Raymond, and gave a weak smile.

She said, 'No, don't take it off! Please put it back on, and do it again, with the mask.' The girl leaned over the table again, but this time to coax him, by grabbing a handful of his crutch, and squeezing hard, 'I liked it.'
Enduring the powerful grip from her small hand, Marvin realised that she didn't even know what Raymond looked like, as he probably kept the mask on both in conversation, and during sex.

What a stroke of luck, Ray would have gone mad, but as it was, he wasn't going to give the game away.

Marvin did not speak, instead because he knew the coast was clear, he did put the mask back on, and followed her back into the other room. Raymond's taste in women was consistent, he thought, as he was about to experience, not just imagine, himself as Raymond.

Chapter 2: Leo

Leo could not wipe the smile off his face. He purred slowly down the High Street, and after two hours he was just as mesmerised by the sound of the engine as when he first picked-up the car. Foreign plates, and not yet available in the UK. It was a car he thought was too good-looking, still smiling, now in the mirror to himself.

The sun rays shone off the surface of the body, picking out every single metallic sparkle of the paintwork, making it dazzle even more.

This type of natural light made it glow and flash with character. As the car prowled on, the warmth was fresh in the April breeze.

The usual sounds of a busy high street, its polluted air and all the milling around by the Saturday morning people, were in the background as Leo gently pushed on the pedal, and smoothly rolled the car down the street. No loud music playing this time, this was his *a capella*.

Heads turned and people waved, but as the five spoke alloys created their own pattern, spinning mesmerically deep in their wheel base, red carpet may as well have been rolled out.

Fresh face and cutting features, Leo only needed to tilt his head at a small angle, and he knew he gave the onlookers that exact pose.

He smiled in such a sure way, his teeth glinted with each showy grin. Not that advertised super-imposed Colgate twinkle, but the real thing. He'd spent a fortune on his teeth.

Right now, Leo could not imagine anybody doing anything better than he did it. He held his dick in his hand as he drove, just resting it on the bulge of his leather trousers, like some sort of precious offering. He was doing four out of the 200 mile an hour top speed. A car like this could drive as slow as it pleased, catch me while you can it says, with a very menacing undercurrent hum from the engine. This is me, Leo thought, and anything else is not a poor imitation, but a jerk.

When he saw a parking space, he slotted the car in with what looked like, felt like and seemed like one movement. He sat back, engine still running.

Lost in a torrent of thoughts, he sighed heavily, and reluctantly killed the motor. He grabbed his matching black portfolio, and slid out of the car, cat-like in motion. He left the hood down.

Leo put on his sunglasses and headed for the agency. He resisted looking back at the car, that was at least for as long as he could. All of three seconds.

His body swayed, from the swell of his head. Leo had gone for a sudden impact look, wearing not only a black leather shirt, but a gold necklace covered all over in diamonds. He didn't pay for it, but it belonged to him.

Sure he knew all about looking the part, and that's what he was doing now. The advert simply read 'Black Extras Required,' but the small print said that this particular job could lead to a serious role, for the right person. Fuck it, why not, thought Leo. Who knew Eddie Murphy, or Wesley Snipes before they were known?

He didn't have any real details about the agency, apart from the gossip he'd heard, and that was from some want-to-be starlet he'd fucked, destined for failure.

Still, what was new? Everything revolved around money, sex, and or power, simple. In fact, they were all the same to him, in as much as they could be traded.

He floated in between the shoppers on the street, dead to the world, alive to himself. When he got to number 245 he entered, and found himself at the reception area.

It turned out that quite a few other people saw the advert, because straight away, he counted about 15 other black guys. He looked around at the plush surroundings, the chandeliers, all the photographs including a couple of familiar faces, the plants, deco furniture, and then the black, grey, and white marble floor that he stood on, and was sure somebody was making a lot of money from hopefuls like him.

What he failed to realise though, was that everybody there noticed him. They watched, feeling privileged that they were in the presence of a movie star. Who else would dress like that?

Cautiously, he approached the receptionist. Leo eyed her as she spoke into a headset, and transferred a call.

'Good morning, how can I help you?' she interjected.

'Er, I've come about the job, I mean come to audition for a part.' Leo spoke quietly, not wanting his entrance to aid or amuse any of the other guys waiting. He felt their stares.

The receptionist had been staring at the diamonds in his necklace, and she wondered if she had heard right, 'For the extras?'

'That's the one,' he said, trying to keep cool. It was getting more absurd by the second.

There was a brief moment of silence while she evaluated the situation. If it was left to her, she'd want to see what this guy could do straight away. Finally she said, 'Have a seat over there, with the others.'

It was a muffled laugh that made him turn around, and he went to take a seat where it came from, with the group.

There was no need for eye contact, he was going to go through with it, even though it wasn't making sense now. Today, he was going to be an average Joe. Tomorrow, tomorrow was a different story altogether.

It had taken Leo 45 minutes to reach Camden from Kensington, a further 35 minutes to go to the lock-up garages, and now he was heading through Kentish Town.

As he drove past Hampstead Heath, he saw a young boy walking a dog, and it meant something to him. When he stopped at the lights, he watched a few other people in the park. They all looked so free to him.

Up along West Hill, and he was in the rich neighbourhood of Highgate Village. Yes, it made him laugh, to think how his boss lived only a stone's throw from Millionaires' Row.

He pulled into the circular gravel driveway, and brought the Porsche alongside a black Mercedes with tinted windows. He saw the wing mirror hanging off the side of the door.

Leo stepped out of Raymond's car, carrying a briefcase in his left hand, and walked towards the two five foot Great Dane statues that framed the reinforced heavy oak door. Of all the things they could have asked him to do, why the hell was he asked to read for the part of a drug dealer. Fucking original, a black drug dealer.

He pressed the doorbell, and heard its chime, along with frenzied barking from the animals inside.

'Hello Leo, on time as usual,' said Ray, as he stood in the doorway, flanked by his two dogs. The temperament of the dogs had always forced Ray to open the door himself.

Leo said, 'Raymond, what's up?'

'Nice man, we did good business last night,' said the big man, as he led Leo through the hallway, and towards one of the sumptuous lounges. As Leo passed the kitchen, he saw for a brief moment what looked like the lower half of a body, with the feet tied-up. Whoever it was, wasn't wearing any shoes, he noticed.

'You're looking good, take a seat over there.' Ray was pointing at his extra large cream leather sofa, but he never took notice of the way people looked, unless they had money for him.

Leo did not say another word, until he had opened the combination satchel, and placed it facing Ray on the glass table. 'I've spun things around, like you said, brought what you wanted, and the cash.'

'Good,' said Ray, 'Rotation is good. Next month, I'll show you the new premises.' He was reaching into the briefcase and checking the serial numbers on the bundles of money. When he finished this, he took one of the eight bags of white powder, pierced it with his little finger, then used it to scoop some into his mouth. 'I love this stuff,' said Raymond, 'OK Leo, the deal is tonight, and I want you to take care of it all. Take the shit, use my car, and don't fuck about. Sell the shit, then drop the money off.' He paused, then said, 'This money here is your bonus. Thirty grand, now you can change your ride.'

Leo said, 'Ray, I don't know what to say. I appreciate it.' He didn't disguise his disappointment. It was long overdue, and was not enough.

Ray said, 'No you don't, you deserve it.'

He said nothing. Leo was tidying the contents of the case, when in walked Harry the Knife Man.

Harry was unaware of the reason for Leo's presence. Raymond didn't want him to know the logistics of any operation. He just cut people up, and that was all.

'Easy Leo, a'wah g'won?'

'Taking care of things, as usual Harry. What about you?' He closed the case. He knew that there was only one reason the Knife Man would be around, but he wanted to know who was tied-up in the kitchen, whether they were dead or alive. It was his job to know, he had to be aware of his boss's friends and enemies, the structure of feeling, and the state of play. There was silence.

'Oh yeah, Warren was making some trouble last night. Bus' my car y'know,' said Ray. 'Get him out of here as you're going. In the kitchen.'

The flimsy way in which the big man spoke made Leo suspicious. What the fuck was he up to now? Another dead fucking body, no warning! He walked away speechless, and went to get the corpse.

Raymond and Harry could be heard laughing in the background. When he reached the kitchen, he saw the body, and bent down so he could raise Warren's slumped head.

A look of horror etched itself across his face. His friend was battered, but still alive.

Leo removed the gag from Warren's mouth, and noted that his breathing was shallow. He untied his hands, and then his feet. There was dried blood from Warren's temple, like dark lava, trailing down to the jaw line. Harry always scarred the ones that he didn't kill for life.

As Leo lifted him up, the texture of Warren's shirt was wet and dry, crispy and soft. More blood thought Leo.

'Warren, I'm taking you home,' said his friend, 'Don't bother to speak until I get you out of here.

He wasn't going to speak. He was barely conscious and still in shock. Leo's voice was the first contact with normality that Warren had had in the last 12 hours. He would never recover from it all, and the mental agony would turn into a rich source of hatred.

Leo supported Warren, draping an arm over his own shoulder, almost carrying him to the front door.

When they got there, Leo raised his hand to the latch, but stopped dead. He turned them around to face the insistent growling from the two pit bulls.

'Ray, come and sort these dogs out, man.' As he shouted this out, he could feel the anger and frustration in his own voice. Yeah, right now he would have liked to shout at Raymond, and ask him what all this madness was about.

It was Ray's hollow laughter that quietened the dogs, as he appeared from the lounge carrying Leo's brief case.

'Get off,' he said to the dogs, and then, 'Leo, as of now, Warren no longer works for us. He's lucky to still be here. Call me later, and keep me posted.'

Leo opened the door, and was leading Warren towards the Porsche. He opened the car, and put him in the passenger side, before returning for the case that Ray was holding. 'Yeah,' he said, 'I'll call you when it's done tonight. The money will be dropped, but I can't make the club tonight, unless you need me?' He wanted the night for himself.

'Na man, I'm busy, that's why you're doing the business,' said Raymond. 'All right, well I'm gone.' 'Get my car cleaned.'

Ray slammed the door full in his face. He went to the car, seething, and wishing once again that he wasn't part of this last sequence of events. Warren was not just part of the crew, he was in the inner circle. He was also a good friend.

As they drove to Kilburn, Warren let a long ten minutes pass before he spoke, then it came out all at once.

'He came out of the blue. Must have been doing 70, easy, on a motorbike, trying to beat the lights, which he never could, while I slowed down at the red. He wouldn't listen. Ray was mad, and didn't care. He uses everything as an excuse and I wonder what I'm supposed to have done? I've been stabbed, slashed in the face, and had a broomstick pushed up my arsehole.'

'Fuck,' said Leo, and it was enough. He wanted to tell Warren how sorry he felt, but it did not seem right speaking in Ray's car. Besides, he had to be careful of what he said about the boss, under any circumstance. Leo kept his thoughts to himself for now.

The rest of the journey was in silence, as he hurried to beat the rush hour traffic, and planned to spend an hour or so while the traffic was at it's peak, talking to Warren at his flat.

It was hard to figure out why Ray had done this, and left the man alive. It was either a mad thing to do, careless, or they shouldn't have touched him in the first place.

Chapter 3: Jenny

Jenny was doing her make-up in front of the dresser in her bedroom. It was another girls' night out as usual on Saturdays.

The fact that she had a six-year-old son did not get in her way. In fact, it never changed her. She was one of those women who at 24 still thought she was a teenager.

She was a pretty, mixed-race girl, and found that men would act foolish in her presence. Jenny was a flirt, and a tease, and if you weren't drawn by her beauty, then you may have found her manner a little raw.

When she finished what she was doing, she went to her walk in closet, and slung a selection of dresses on the bed, excited at the prospect of what to wear to titillate the boys tonight. She loved her men to beg, if not with their mouths, then with their eyes. The father of her children no longer did this, and in an unspoken way it gave them a mutual acceptance of the situation. However, it did not mean that there was no feelings between them. The magic had gone, that was all. Despite being separated, they still made love.

The doorbell rang, and having just slipped onto a Versace number, Jenny thought her friend Debbie had arrived early. The dress she wore was long and see through. The bell rang again.

'All right,' she yelled, and headed for the door with no shoes on.

When she got there and opened it, Jenny was angry, and at the same time surprised to see Leo. 'What do you want?'

'Watch your mouth,' he said, 'If you start it like this, how the hell can we ever have a normal friggin' conversation?'

'We have not got anything to say to each other today! It's not the end of the month! It's not time for you to see your son!'

What Jenny meant was, I'm getting ready to go out.

'Look, I'm not here to argue, OK, and now I've told you.' Which meant shut-up already.

'What's the matter Leo, have you come to fuck me then?' She emphasised the word fuck, making it sound rough, but she had never turned him down.

He didn't answer, and walked past her into the flat, as she stood in the doorway, with her hands on her hips.

Leo heard the front door slam, and he said, 'Is that how you are going out tonight? Do you know what you look like?'

'Leo, don't start this shit. Come on, you know I don't care what you think. You also know that I paid for it with your money. So what's it got to do with you?' She looked at his leather trousers and shirt, eyed his gold necklace with the diamond stones. 'You look disgusting.'

'Where is he?'

'Asleep,' she said.

'I've just come from Warren's house, I need a drink.'

'You know where the fridge is.'

'You know sometimes, you've got no class, and no manners.'

'And you're prince charming himself. Look, I'm getting ready to go out, and LJ's nan is coming to look after him. Don't be here when she arrives, I couldn't handle that scene.' Her mother hated Leo. She did not like him much before they split, and now, she just seemed to shout at him whenever she saw him.

Leo walked to the kitchen and on the way he had a flash-back of Warren's feet, tied as they were with no shoes on at Ray's. 'Well it's nice of you to organize your Saturday night as usual.'

This was not the time for Jenny to explain to Leo that she did not like the way she had become. He'd heard it all before anyway. In her life now, things happened as they happened, and she was resigned to this.

This was how she had driven him out of his mind, and he had hit her, and put her in hospital. When he had started, he couldn't stop.

Just that one time in his whole life had he hit a woman. He had been working, and was away for lengthy periods of time. Jenny had relations with someone, and Leo found out.

Returning with a beer in his hand, his favourite, Coors Extra Gold, he went and sat down in the living room.

The flat was quite small, but Leo had decorated it with the help of a good interior designer. Jenny even suspected that he was seeing the girl at the time, but had no proof it.

He turned on the television, and flicked through to Sky Sport, wanting to see if there was anything on about the fight that would be shown in the later hours, pay-per-view.

She now stood in the doorway that led to the lounge. From here she watched him, thinking how tired he looked, and half wishing that they were going to spend the night together.

'Look, Leo, if you need to talk to someone, you've come to the wrong place.'

He made no comment. The last hour at Warren's place had got to him. Leo had decided it was time. For what exactly, he was not sure.

'Jenny,' he said, 'We've been apart a year and a half, and for what it's worth, like most things in my life, I'm not sure what to do about it.'

'Leo,' she began, but stopped. 'Look, we've been through this before, why bring it up again?' 'Come here,' he said to her.

Matthew Williams' work, whether prose, poetry, painting or multi-media, never rests in the mainstream—he prefers the experimental, adventurous, unconventional route to art. He won second prize in both poetry and fiction sections of the 1998 *Prison Writing* Competition, has had exhibitions of his visual work shown in Liverpool, and has written an as-yet unpublished novel, *The Engines of Babel*. Sentenced to five discretionary life sentences in 1989 at the age of 19, he was confined to Special Security Units after an unauthorised but much-publicised sabbatical from Parkhurst in 1995. Here, he writes from an unusual perspective . . .

Virgo Intacta

Matthew Williams

We moved next to the prison when I was seven. It frightened me at first, staring at me through its sewn-up eyelids. But Dad said I'd just have to bloody well get used to it as James (my elder brother) had first choice of the back bedrooms, and there was no way *he* (Dad, I mean) was going to look at that monstrosity every morning. So I did instead. Actually, it wasn't that bad. The only bit I could see was the top two rows of cell windows, about a hundred yards distant, over this dirty big wall. But still, I was afraid. At first, that is.

For weeks I kept my curtains and window shut, as if the prisoners' eyes were going to reach out through their bars and over the wall and sneak into my room on long stalks and do things to me. My mum said I was a silly little girl and made me open the window and curtains up. She did make me a net curtain though, to calm my childish fears. What do you think, she said, they give them all telescopes in there?

That's when I had the idea. For a telescope, I mean. I bought one off my friend Julie for five pounds and a Gameboy cartridge, then set it up through the net curtains to watch *them* instead. It was fun at first, even James wanted to see, but after hours at the eyepiece, all we ever saw were some blurry faces spitting and throwing bits of food out through the cell bars, so we just gave up out of boredom.

It was months later that I saw him. He must have just been put in there, I'm sure I would have noticed him earlier otherwise. It was a Saturday night, and I'd got up for a wee (I'd not been well all day) and through the net curtain I saw a light on in a cell. It surprised me, because it was after two in the morning, and I thought they all had to go to sleep after a certain time. I peered secretly out at him, sure that he'd stayed up to watch me, frightened that he could see me even in my dark room.

Then I got angry—*he* was the prisoner, not me! So I got my telescope and focussed it in on his silhouette.

I was shocked by what I saw. He was so, so young. Almost a boy, really. And his eyes were closed. He was frowning and I thought I saw his lips move a bit. He had really short hair. Actually, he looked a lot like James. Behind him, brightly lit, I could see the corner of a painting, orange and red shapes, all swirling about. I wished I could see all of it. I looked away from the telescope, the boy prisoner a distant shadow.

Was he a murderer? Did the ghost of his victim haunt him? I watched him for another half hour, willing him to open his eyes, but he never did. He was still up at three, when I went back to bed.

The next week, he was there again. Saturday night, backlit in his window, staring out at the world from which he had been exiled. The boy prisoner, and a new painting, just visible over his shoulder.

Blue this time—the corner of some skyscape, I imagined. In my telescope he loomed large and silent, a mask inscrutable. Again, I wondered what colour his eyes were.

One by one through the evening, the other cell windows blinked off their dim lights, leaving his the only beacon lit on that land-locked concrete ship, burning away into the small hours, where fatigue
crept up on me and carried me to bed.

Funny now when I look back, but I never told anyone about my discovery, I don't know why. For months I watched him, keeping silent vigil with him each Saturday night, my scope now fixed onto his sole position. For a few weeks I tried to glimpse him at other times, but then I changed my mind. Seeing him throw rubbish or spit from his cell would spoil our secret. He was different. Special. His weekly beacon became a fixed, unistellar constellation, and I became the dedicated astronomer, eager to map its hidden face.

I grew up with that constellation. The Painter, I called it, the boy prisoner's wall changing often as a new canvas adorned it. I wished I could see more of them, but our rooms were angled such that I never saw more than a fragment. His existence, like his paintings, the corners of an occulted jigsaw.

When I was 12, our house was burgled and my telescope was stolen. We were all in a state for weeks at the violation of our home, especially Mum. I hated The Painter then, he was a burglar too, I supposed, and so on Saturday me and James shouted swear words at the prison until Dad came up and asked what the bloody hell we were playing at.

A week later, I guiltily whispered an apology to the lonely cell, my closeness to him lost until I got a new telescope. One with a bigger lens. It brought us closer together.

On my fourteenth birthday there was an escape form the prison, and I was terrified that the boy had broken out, having seen me watch him, and now he was coming for revenge. James and Dad even helped in the search, but my fears proved groundless. That Saturday night, he was at his window as usual. I sighed with relief and sent him a smile, not realising that he probably dreamed of escape, and fleeing that concrete cube.

It was ages till I used my telescope again. It was a Christmas Eve, and I was 17 and a half. James had thrown a party for his college friends, Mum and Dad having trusted the house to him for the evening. That night, in my room, I lost my virginity to Alan Hughes, a boy from my sixth form. I was drunk, and it hurt, and Alan just went home afterwards. I spent the whole night crying in the dark, listening to the music downstairs. It was like I'd ceased to exist, fallen out of the real world into somewhere frightening and unknown. When it went quiet, with everyone gone, I went to the window. The Painter was there, as he'd always been.

I dusted off my telescope, and looked at the boy's face. What I saw shocked me, and I began to cry once more. But this time I was crying for him. The boy had become a man. His face looked lined and old, his hair had thinned round his temples, his whole demeanour had sunk, somehow, as if the weight of the concrete had broken him.

I realised at that moment he had been in that same room every night and every day for over ten years. Ten years of emptiness. Of loneliness. I thought of the holidays I'd had, the Christmases, the birthdays . . . and through all that time, the boy had been growing older and more alone in that one bare room.

I wept, and felt the blood between my legs. Had he ever known a woman? Had he over known that ultimate intimacy? I pulled back the curtains and put on the light, silhouetting myself. Soon after I was sure I felt his eyes upon me, my naked body exposed for him. I stayed up with him all that night, until dawn faded The Painter's light, and I saw him disappear from his window.

I never saw him again. That night there had been no painting on his wall, and I hope in my heart it was a sign that he was due to be released. Wherever he now is. I wonder if he still paints. And if he does, whether his memory of our night together has ever found expression on canvas.

Virgo Intacta © Matthew Williams 2000

There can be few prisoners who have not let their minds wander and their imagination take them beyond the walls and away from reality. In 'Not Today', **Stephen Barraclough,** a lifer in HMP Kingston, looks at the dangers of going too far . . .

Not Today

Stephen Barraclough

I always look forward to the summer because that's when the evening exercise periods begin. We have a reasonably large playing field to walk around, its perimeter edged by a concrete path. And it's my habit to walk around this path between six and eight each evening, Monday to Thursday, but only in summer, of course.

There are usually two wardens out there who walk around during those hours but it's not usual for them to bother us. Sometimes they almost seem like inmates themselves—the way they talk, smile and laugh. Sometimes I even wonder what they're like beneath their uniform.

• • •

This evening I am out there walking. It is lovely and warm and the prison garden party has cultivated a variety of colourful flowers, which are out on parade. In this usually drab environment the flowers act as a potent reminder. Throughout the years one becomes more and more immune to the activities and the splendour of what is on the other side of the tall grey walls. Until, that is, one sees the flowers.

You might wonder what I think about while I'm walking around. Some time ago I began playing a sort of game. Well, it started as a game but it has become more than that now. Has begun to take on a more serious aspect. It becomes that I am no more walking around the exercise field at this establishment in Hampshire, than the Queen of England is out begging on the streets of London.

No, I'm not on this field any longer. In fact I am now walking through the streets of Harrow. In fact to tell you the truth, I've been walking along these streets every evening for the past fortnight. Of course, it's still a novel experience to see the shops, and the proprietors with whom I was so familiar. And I've met old friends and even bumped into my sister once or twice since the game became serious. In fact I took her for a quiet drink in the pub up on the hill in Harrow one night. We had a lovely evening and I got her a taxi home at the end of it. And both my parents are alive, well and extremely happy. Mother's had a bouquet of flowers, while my father was very pleased with the vintage bottle of port I took round the other evening.

On Wednesday, that was. The night before, I met my sister.

Tonight though, I am going to visit my girlfriend. And that's the odd thing. . . that though I want to see her more than anyone, I've never yet made it to her door.

Which is strange—because in the game everything is possible. I can win the Lottery. I can arrive at my parents' house in a Rolls-Royce. Everyone I visit is happy and contented. However, when it comes to changing fact to fiction in relation to my girlfriend, it just doesn't seem to work—but I am determined it will this evening.

The walk to my girlfriend's house is a long one, as she lives at one end of a main road, and I always enter from the other end. I stare at the familiar houses as I pass them. I've seen them a thousand times before, of course—though that was years ago.

I reach the roundabout, with the four busy roads leading off, and I half run and partly scramble my way across. The cars are racing off in all directions behind me. Now I walk quicker as I can't think straight in the sort of din they make.

The car noise.

Here's her front gate. Opening it, I walk down her path and, although a sudden nervousness comes on me, I knock on the door anyway. It opens and there she is.

The nervousness within me increases in the way she is looking at me. It is not a friendly look, neither is it particularly hostile, but a sort of sullen bored look over her face.

I speak and her voice in replying is far different from how I remember it. She seems nervous herself. So I think of something else to say, and this time as she answers a man appears from behind her. She stiffens at his presence, and I wonder what he is doing in her house. Standing there behind her as if he lives there himself. Now it is I who suddenly feels the outsider. And then it all becomes painfully obvious; the reason why I kept putting off this particular journey. I want to walk away, but will feel humiliated in doing so, and this prevents me from going as I know I should.

And I know I can't leave without some parting verbal shot at the figure behind her. When he hears it he pushes her aside and lunges towards me. He is bigger and more powerful than I am, and begins half-pushing, half-pulling me up the path back towards the open gate

I am struggling and, although I don't know why, I begin to scream. A scream which grows louder and louder because it is coming from deep within me. It is not just aimed at him, or her, but at this establishment I'm in. And lots of other things as well. The screaming contains hate and bitterness and resentment and fear and frustration. It is as though I am trying to exorcise from within me all these things. And as the noise of my screaming rises and rises an odd thing happens. A man in a uniform suddenly appears and then another. And then more . . . .

• • •

It is quiet here, in the prison hospital. I have been here a while now. I had to appear before the prison governor the morning following my outburst. It was called an 'adjudication'. The governor was quite stern to begin with. He told me he was considering bringing a charge of assault against me. Apparently I had lashed out at one of the warders on the field and struck him on the mouth.

I told the governor about my game and my journeys, and that I had accidentally struck the warder while struggling outside my girlfriend's front door.

At this the governor's manner changed. He adjourned the adjudication for me to be examined by the prison doctor who, in turn, recommended the assault charge and the adjudication be dismissed. This seems to have happened, because I have heard no more about it.

So now I lie in bed and take my daily medication, which makes me feel sluggish and tired a lot of the time. But I see the doctor three mornings a week and I always ask him when I will be allowed to go out on the field again. I have to get back to Harrow and my life.

His reply is always the same, though. He smiles and slowly shakes his head 'Not today,' he tells me. 'Not today.'

Not Today © Stephen Barraclough 2000

Looking at Life was begun while Simon Scott was on remand in Belmarsh, waiting to be sentenced to life imprisonment. Up-to-date research on the experience of lifers is hard to find, particularly regarding the pre-sentence and immediately post-sentence periods. Here, the author describes his innermost attempts to look forward, to the day he is due to be sentenced, and then to contemplate how he might cope with the years ahead.

Looking at Life

Simon Scott

One

Just for half-an-hour there it felt like life was normal. I was lying in my bed reading the 'introductions' adverts in the weekend paper to my cell-mate and we were having a laugh at the expense of others: you know, when an ad says 'tall, curvaceous lady' which basically means a 'big fat bird'. Pretty sad affair for a Saturday night but Frank and I have spent about 68 out of the last 72 hours together and I guess we'd exhausted most of the in-cell entertainment options. Easter holidays may be full of hectic weekend escapes, traffic jams and chocolate in the city that surrounds us, but in this corner of London they are about staff shortages and bang-up.

As we mulled over our respective picks of the week's lonely *Guardian* readers (Frank's was 39, likes fags and white wine, mine was 39 and into ski-ing and red wine) we both slipped into Fantasy Land and just for a short while wondered if we could ever meet these compatible companions. We joked about how we'd reply, how we would introduce ourselves, when would we have to tell the truth. Frank's prospect was looking for a 'classy man' and he wondered whether a Class A man would be a reasonable substitute—would she wait eight years, and would supplying bulk heroin qualify him as a 'profess. M'?

My potential partner's ad caught my eye because she was looking for a man between 45 and 55 so I should fit right into that bracket by the time I'm able to meet for that 'informal meal leading to poss. relationship'. By then she'll be looking for someone in their seventies. Most people, including myself, would think it extremely foolish for me to contemplate release from prison, never mind building a relationship, but my only hope for freedom is in my mind at the moment, I can't even imagine what walking down a road will feel like. The only certain thing about my future is that it's not going to bear any similarity to my past.

After eleven months on remand I'm finally looking forward to a date when I can go up and be given my sentence. Somehow I think things will change, that suddenly people will take an interest in me, help me plan my time in prison, talk to me about where I would like to spend my time, discuss the options that I'll have available to me to address my offending behaviour. Care? Should they care?

But nothing is going to change on May 19. I won't suddenly become guilty of a crime just because I plead guilty to it in court. I've been guilty from the second I committed the crime. I won't be given any indication of how long I will spend in prison—I'll 'just' be given a life sentence. I won't be sent to a lifers' prison, I'll be brought back here and locked up in the same room I left that morning. If I'm lucky the officers on the wing might be told that I've just been 'lifed off' and perhaps they'll wish me all the best and tell me that I can make it through.

Or maybe I'll go to pieces in court, blub all the way back to reception, be given Valium and be carted off to the hospital wing. Shit, I hope the old advice that 'it won't hit you straightaway' proves to be true—I don't want to spend my first convicted night with the fraggles, doped out, after all these months clean from drugs. For fuck's sake, please let me be strong. I spent a week in the hospital wing at Wandsworth when I first came in and I was begging to be allowed into the main prison. C wing was a breeze compared to the mind fuck that waits in the hospital. The insomniac shoplifter who wants Valium for breakfast, the far-gone black pensioner who wants his door opened because his taxi is here, the whining alkies and smackheads puking and choking, the zombie shuffling for his breakfast barefoot.

Just give me a single cell on a normal wing and lock me in. Please don't put me in the hospital. Bang up I can do.

Two

I'd been shitting myself all week but Thursday I was strangely calm. I think the relief of having something to do saved me from my nerves. I was determined to take all my essential kit to court so that I wouldn't panic if I wasn't brought back to the same cell. Of course, officially I was being discharged from the prison so I was required by prison rules to take all my kit with me. Because this would have amounted to several huge sacks of books and letters, I opted against it. Ironically, the wing staff at Belmarsh are quite happy to save your cell for you when you attend court as long as you take all your kit with you. Kind of defeats the object of saving the cell as you turn into a human snail for the day.

So I packed my kit, prepared for the potential hospital visit, and hid my non-essential kit in the cupboard. What amounts to essential kit for a prospective lifer? Just about everything really. On one occasion I was advised by a cellmate at Wandsworth just to leave all my kit in the cell, that all I needed to do was advise the wing staff politely that I would like to be returned to the same cell that evening and they would comply. Since then I've ignored all advice given to me by inmates. I returned that evening and politely requested the same south facing dwelling as I had left that morning. Not a hope. I tried pleading. I tried explaining that I felt suicidal and that my cell-mate had saved me from myself many times. This being interpreted as a threat, brought me only a four letter rebuke. So to me my essential kit is every bit of paper, every letter, every photo I have ever received from outside. All my toiletries, all my clothes, all my books. You'd wonder what else this would leave but I can assure you it's just possible to accumulate crap in prison. The game of deciding how much to take, what I could live without, what I could easily carry without losing pounds to sweat in the sprint to reception, occupied my mind for a while at least.

Friday a.m. was the familiar old routine, down to reception for the usual stripshow for the officers. I wonder if they enjoy it, whether gay prison officers always request reception duty? Everyone else off the houseblock was going to Cat C prisons and was moaning about how they would have to wait until after the induction process to get a telly. Could be as long as two weeks. Wow, they might miss Euro 2000. Arseholes, I only just had an outside shot at Euro 2016.

After the peep show Securicor kindly gave me a lift up to the Old Bailey—I was relieved as reception process was a bit slow and I was going to miss my train. It was a drab, damp morning. The sweatbox, not famed for its comfort, was sticky and causing my court suit to become somewhat crumpled. I doubted whether my appearance would do me any favours on this day anyway but it would have been pleasant to feel I had at least one good aspect. Due to surplus numbers of high security prisoners being despatched to the Bailey on this day we had to do a couple of laps of St. Paul's in the rain. Any thoughts I didn't have about trying a suicide leap over the dock of the court were immediately dropped when I saw the armed police out in force for the Cat A men coming along behind us. Not that the Bailey would be the place to jump the dock but whenever I'm out of prison, even in a secure van, I always secretly harbour thoughts of not going back.

But I did go back. One life sentence to the good. This seemed to be a popular choice for the judges that day at the 'fairest court in the land'. In my case he had no choice so I couldn't really moan. On return to the prison I had no real problem avoiding the hospital wing—all that stress for nothing. All I had to do was sign a book. I don't know why I had to sign it or what I was signing, it doesn't pay to ask that sort of question. Presumably I was promising not to kill myself, or at least to absolve my guardians of any blame if I did.

All I felt was tired and stressed as I returned to the wing. I managed to have the first confrontation with an officer since coming to prison a year before. Stupidly, I ask if I can 'phone my mother to tell her that I've just got a life sentence but that I still feel normal and sane. I get a refusal. I respond in a slightly stroppy manner. 'I haven't asked for one thing in a year in this place. I get lifed off and ask for a 'phone call and you refuse.' Reply: 'Do you want some hot water? A sharp 'No' cuts off my nose and I retire for the evening and slam the door shut myself, depriving the officer of what must surely be his favourite duty of the day.

After the weekend I move to Houseblock One, a single cell. Lifers. No screw makes any reference at all to my sentence. In fact when I complain that the cell is cold, the response is 'What do you want me to do?' It will be a long time before the POA follows everyone else and starts thinking of 'customer satisfaction'—when I suggest that I could be moved to a warmer cell I'm told that I shouldn't even have this cell since it is a single and I'm not a lifer. Now, I don't expect any screw to know me well after only a couple of days on the wing but there are only three things on my door—my name, number and the word 'LIFE'. I can assure you that the last of these three is not to indicate that I still have some left in me—or is it?

Three

Well, almost a week to the minute since I was sentenced to life and I shed my first tear for myself. Yep, a tear for me, no pretence in these watery eyes. I've not even done a fraction of my sentence, in fact I don't even have a clue as to how long life will be for me, and I'm already overawed by the sheer size of it. I could moan about the effectiveness of incarceration, about how it doesn't do anyone any good but until I finish my tariff it's purely a punishment period so I think that kind of excludes me from moaning, or at least it devalues it. Of course I would moan, I'm being punished.

It's quite strange, the average person wouldn't look in my cell and perceive it as a punishment. Nobody is beating the soles of my feet, *Midnight Express* style, I don't have to clean my toilet with a toothbrush, I don't really have to do very much. Okay, the food is classified by Amnesty International as torture but then it has been pointed out to me that if I don't like it I can always buy food from the canteen. The punishment, if you are human, is entirely self-administered. It's what your mind does to you in long quiet periods of solitude that hurts. Because it completely refuses to let go. Of memories, of emotions, of feeling. And this isn't a suitable place to hold onto any of those.

The smart con could be the one who doesn't have photographs on his notice-board, who doesn't make phone-calls or receive letters. For the rest of us these are just visual and aural stimuli which lead to the pain of memories. I can never figure out which hurt more—the good memories or the bad ones. They are all so fresh at the moment, it's only been a year.

I'm looking forward to them fading away. Or am I? Although this will make day-to-day life easier I will have lost my most treasured possessions, for them to be replaced by inferior prison-made ones. Maybe this osmosis, this seeping away of old memories just happens slowly over time and before you really notice all you can remember is prison. The attachment I have to my past is inevitably going to lead to suffering. I don't need to be a Buddha to figure that one out. So, is the solution one of the ascetic monk—remove all the material objects and you will defeat the spiritual desire—do I need to remove the physical reminders to try and stop my memories from floating up into my consciousness and destroying my peace of mind?

Easy ways to do this are of course available. I'm in a maximum security prison where all letters, parcels and visits are closely and rigorously monitored, X-rayed and subject to sniffer dog attack so needless to say there is plenty of smack and puff around every wing. The alternative to chemical Nirvana is spiritual Nirvana and perhaps meditative bliss would be a good way for me to channel my energies. The problem is that each of these mechanisms puts a level of abstraction between me and my past, deadening the pain but also killing the emotions. Removing me from society more effectively than prison could ever do. It's a cliché but they only lock up our bodies, maybe the reason that smack is allowed in here is an attempt to lock up our minds. Me, I've never been much of a one for conspiracy theories or opiates. About as useless as each other in the long run.

So, if I follow the path to the cessation of suffering by removing the link between my surroundings and my emotions, how do I cope when I'm eventually thrown back onto the street? Okay, we all know this is going to be a fucking long time but I do worry that any survival mechanisms I develop now are going to need to be carefully scrutinised for their long-term effects. Obviously, if I took Route H I wouldn't have to worry about being on the street too long and I could leave my toothbrush here. If I go with the meditation option can I just flip back to my normal self on exit and go looking for a beer and a shag or am I destined to spend the rest of my days in a retreat continuing my solitary confinement?

Surely there is some middle way here—a route to avoid the pain of incarceration whilst remaining sane, drug-free and close to those that we love and miss. I doubt it. If there was, fewer people would jump on the smack train. For a long-term prisoner I suppose the hope must be that they can avoid the detox in the same way that GIs avoided the detox on their return from Vietnam. The drug-taking being so tied into the environment that there are few psychological problems following the release from the environment and the cessation of drug taking. I would say drug abuse but I don't see it that way—what are opiates if not pain killers? If taking them is abusing them, then would someone please explain what the fuck they are intended for?

No. Aside from the two extremes of meditation and heroin, I don't yet believe there is a middle way to avoid pain in prison whilst remaining human. That's why the punishment works, for those of us who avoid taking drugs that is. Not that many people perhaps. But to me, to be able to fit back into society we need to retain the ability to feel our own pain and appreciate the pain of others. So I guess this stretch isn't going to be so easy.

Looking at Life © Simon Scott 2000

Motives are not always what they seem; sometimes they never become fully apparent. This is the subject area **Michael Williamson** of HMP Channings Wood in the following two short stories.

Reflections

Michael Williamson

You have to believe me. I have tried, but even I have run out of patience. I cannot put up with him anymore. I'm going to cut the guy up and leave him scarred, good and proper.

I'm sick of his voice, that nasal whine that grates on my nerves every time he opens his mouth. I'm sick of the repetitive, predictable crap that he talks. Name a crime, he's done it. Name a body, he knows him. Fuck, even the lies he tells aren't true.

I'm sick and tired of his scrounging, 'Got any units, mate? Got any skins? Any sugar, my man?' His party piece has got to be, 'Got any Jimmy Boyle, mate, you know, Jimmy Boyle, foil?' Yeah, I know, you smacked up spineless prick, fuck off and die.

I'm sick of having to share my space with the dirty bastard. The guy must have an allergy to water because he avoids the showers like the plague, and his breath smells like a sewer. It must be to do with all the shit that comes out of his mouth on a daily basis.

I'm finished listening to all his bitching and moaning, 'I'm innocent, my man—I was set up by the pigs to get me off the scene, they hate me, man.' I can understand them—I hate you too. I've come to the end of my tether, what with having to tolerate his attitude. He's a piss-poor petty thief, yet he swans about like he's one of the great train robbers. They weren't so great, fuck me, they got caught too.

It winds me up, but I have to laugh when he portrays himself as an idyllic family man. Shut up mate, I know your girlfriend, you wife-beating beast. You couldn't fight a man if your life depended on it. Fight with me then, your life WILL depend on it. I'm going to fucking kill you. I've waited and at last your time has come.

Get ready to take one final bow, boy, because the show is nearly over. Scared? Oh, no, not this one. Rock solid. Rock fucking solid? Don't make me laugh. Rock solid bully, maybe. Well, pal, it's my turn to be the bully now, here I come, ready or not.

I must admit I'm proud of the tool that I have made, took me ages to melt and work it so that two razor blades fitted into the handle. Makes it nigh on impossible to sew the cut up. I can't take chances with this one, can I? If a job's worth doing, then its worth doing right, right? I'll need to time this right so that there's no chance of anyone finding him. Last thing I need is some do-gooder interfering. I'm getting butterflies in the pit of my belly as the time draws nearer. Patience my man, patience.

Bingo, bang up at last, just him and I, all on our lonesome. Time to get down to business, but before I get busy I pause to have one last thought about things to myself. Maybe I'm being too hard on the guy, maybe I should give him yet another second chance. Maybe . . . then again, maybe not.

No, I've decided, this waste of skin must die. My mind is racing as I think about what his face will look like as the last semblance of life drains out of him. I wonder what thoughts will be going through his tiny mind. Butterflies again. Will he scream or cry? Will he try to cling to life, holding on like an unwanted lover or for once in his life will he take it like a man? Soon see, eh?

Amidst the chaos of my thoughts, one thing is crystal clear. Mine is the last face that he will ever see. Then, lights out and goodnight to another oxygen thief. Show's over, no encore required, thank you.

I've done dozens of guys before, birds too, but this one seems almost like a personal crusade to me. One last thing I need to do before I begin. In an attempt to gouge out some kind of reaction to what I am going to do I look into the cell mirror. No reaction. None whatsoever.

I take a good long, honest look into my eyes. I'd recommend it to any man, it gives you a good sense of perspective on life, or death. It gives you an unbiased look at who you really are. Give it a try sometime.

'This is going to hurt you more than it's going to hurt me', I say aloud and then I begin cutting . . .

Epilogue

The unfortunate officer who found the body in the morning looks like a broken man. It wasn't so much the blood or the ferocity of the wounds that were inflicted on the body that was causing his emotional turmoil. It was the feeling of being overwhelmed by the sense of both guilt and grief, deeper than any feelings he had ever experienced in his life time.

He had noticed the prisoner, it was hard not to, and he had suspected that the guy had problems, but this? This was tragic. He wished that he had spoken to him more, surely there was something he could have said? No amount of training prepared him for this. He couldn't help feeling he could have done more to help.

He did offer to get one of the listeners to come and see him, but alas he had refused. He even refused when asked if he wanted a cellmate rather than be cooped up on his own. The guy was adamant that he was not sharing a cell with anyone.

He wonders what could have been going on in such a young man's head to make him commit suicide so violently. It would be a question that he would ask himself time and time again, it came with the job. It was also a question which would be destined to remain unanswered forever.

• • •

A Librarian's Tale: All For Promotion

Four down, one to go. Then she was the winner. She was enjoying this. Never before in her life had she felt freedom or power to equal what she was experiencing at present. Not even the joys of cross-referencing or re-checking the Author/Titles came close to this. She'd managed to 'eliminate' the competition easily so far. She'd had enough time in her lunch breaks to study various strategies in order to prepare herself more than adequately and looking back, in retrospect, her choices of 'Military Tactics' and 'How to . . . be ruthless but liked' had so far proved to be good choices. Perfect almost.

No more Miss Wishy-Washy the Librarian. Now she was the mental equivalent of Robo-Cop. Dedicated to the job in hand; namely the elimination of the opposition. Calm and focused, no more nervous dilly-dallying for her. And ruthless: only one of the city library's employees stood to be promoted once they had won this paintball skirmish. She was totally determined that it would be her. In fact it was a certainty. She just loved the gun she'd chosen. And she'd chosen it all by herself. With knowledge, of course, from a book of firearms that she'd read at her place of employment. She adored working at the city library. The smells, the noise (or lack of it) and the sense of peace, tranquillity and order. She had to win. It was her God-given right, her destiny . . .

• • •

Game on . . . She inched forward slowly, covering the places where her opponent could hide. It was dimly lit inside the maze but she'd done her research (in her own time of course) and decided that infra-red goggles would give her an added advantage. After all, wasn't this exercise about showing initiative? So far it seemed to have paid off, because now there was only her and Kevin left, and no way was she going to lose her promotion to some wannabe author who did nothing but check books in, check books out. As she crept forwards she caught a glimpse of her 'prey' in the grey-green luminance of the goggles. He was up ahead and just about to turn down a passage in an attempt to avoid her again. She could see the red liquid on his leg from where she had hit him earlier. As he limped away she thought, 'You're overdue, time to pay your fine.' She often had thoughts like this. How it irritated her when members of the City Library returned books and acted like they were innocent of any crime.

She followed the sole survivor around the turn in the maze. She could see him panicking and he was beginning to hyperventilate. He still had his gun, she noticed, and she hoped that it was empty. The paintballs stung and left an awful mess when they hit you. She was closing fast now, creeping silently closer to her next 'kill'. Kevin stood still, stationary, as if unsure where to go next. Fifteen yards . . . ten . . . five . . .

'Hands up!' she barked. 'But first put your weapon down'. Kevin obeyed. More adrenalin, more power.

'Please don't,' whispered Kevin, 'I don't even want the promotion'.

'You know that I have to shoot you to win, Kevin,' she said calmly. 'I *need* that promotion, it's nothing personal.'

Kevin stood silent, his eyes shining in the dim light cast by the lights on the maze wall. He was crying. She raised her gun and pointed it at his head.

'Goodbye Kevin, it's been nice working with you.'

Before he could reply or plead further she pulled the trigger and Kevin's head exploded against the wall in a kaleidoscopic mixture of flesh, bone and grey mush. She was glad of her choice of bullets that exploded on impact. Also learned about from the book on firearms from the library. Well, that was that then.

•   •   •

All she had to do now was find her way back through the maze to the exit. She walked back through the maze, past the losers and felt good about herself. She was a little surprised when she opened the exit door to find an armed response unit waiting for her, rifles aimed and ready. She was sure she recognised one of them. In fact she was sure he had a copy of *Five Go Mad in Dartmoor* that was nearly a fortnight overdue. As she obeyed the order to put down the weapon and placed her hands upon her head she made a mental note to have a word with that particular officer concerning his overdue book.

Reflections and *A Librarian's Tale: All for Promotion* © Michael Williamson 2000

Darren Blanchflower, a lifer in HMP Durham, began to write in the Close Supervision Unit at Woodhill. This is his first published work.

Poems by Darren Blanchflower

Home

The fresh, clean air, of home, a pleasant memory.
The market place, busy and noisy, but very welcoming,
With cheerful banter, warm laughter, my home.

Mother's house, my childhood home,
with everything in it's place.
My old room, stereo silent, with records stacked,
Waiting for my return home.

The caring neighbours, all the same,
apart from the added years.
The old school-friends, now grown and married,
The precious life-blood of my home.

The atmospheric pubs and dance clubs, a meeting place,
For friends, some long-standing, others new,
Old loves, new loves, school-time crushes,
All there, at home.

Detecting Defectives

Tall man, black coat, black hat, sunglasses,
a burrower of human flesh,
a hunter of the broken.

He looks everywhere, for oddities, an ugly face,
for a cold glint of eye,
or a sneer of mouth.

Listening for bizarre talk, either mumbling,
screeching or shouting,
all symptoms of the diseased.

Reaching into their filth, finding a grip, pulling in,
Deeper than deep,
then melting their souls.

One Last Dash for Freedom

Spot-light searching the blackness,
hunting out the killer.
The killer blends with shadows,
waiting for his chance.

Run, and run fast, escape from the cage,
He doesn't look back, not once.

Shrilling alarm bells ring out, piercing the
Night-time sky, then the bark of dogs,
They join the fray, to hunt the hunted hunter.

He starts to tire, his legs feeling weak, his time, it's
Running out.
He clambers into a hedge-row, cold, tired, and scared,
Trying to be invisible.

The dogs smell his scent, they bark and snarl,
The guards know he's close, excitement builds,
Then the dogs are released, and they charge in,
The take-down is on.

Though he feels the teeth bite and tear his flesh,
He struggles not, despair and failure too strong,
For he knows his last grasp for freedom is gone,
And a life-time of incarceration awaits.

The Prisoner

'Shut those doors' a voice shouts out, locking men
and women both in and out.
In a room that's made of stone, out of a house, that was
Once their home.

And where we now find ourselves living, which is no more
than a human zoo, really is not very pleasant, and you don't get
a 'room' with a view.

We travel on a conveyer belt, everyday the same,
Unlock, breakfast, bang-up, away we go again,
Exercise, bang-up, dinner, then banged-up once again,
Then we're unlocked at tea-time, then behind the door again,
Then that's it till morning, where it all starts over again.

The days seem to blur and fade away, without us noticing
They're gone, until another Christmas comes around, or
Another birthday comes.

As the years start to pass, grey hairs, wrinkles, or baldness begin
To leave their mark,
Memories, our only companions, reminding us who we are,
And of the lives that we once had, that now, have sadly passed.

When this experience finally ends,
through our release, or sadly,
Death, those years of lonely solitude,
we can finally lay to rest.

An Acceptance

My tears run free, burning my skin, guilt, sadness, fear,
my antagonists.
Remembering bad times, that I once believed were good,
Bringing shame to cleanse my mind.

All my victims, of emotional and physical pain,
They patiently wait, for justice, for the truth.
I can admit my guilt, but my reasons for my crimes,
They are meaningless, because there can never be a justified reason,
Ever.

This punishment, I freely accept, for crimes such as mine, I need
Punishing.
All I ask and wish for, is forgiveness, from my family, my victims,
Their families, and my god.

I hope for my freedom one day, to right just some of my wrongs,
To explain face to face my actions, to my victims.
Then, to live quietly, peacefully and honestly, with my family.

If any good could come from incarceration, mine is maturity,
Honesty, and guilt.
To know and accept what I did was wrong, and to change.
Then to lay the past to rest, to move forward.

Moral Tales

Moral Tales

This is a story about loyalty, about standing for one's principles in the face of personal danger. The author, **Simon Tasker** of The Wolds, describes his route to publication: 'Since an early age I've evolved through foster parents, kid's homes, YOIs and prison. Reading was always a good means of escaping my immediate surroundings, whilst feeding my imagination. Facing another sentence just before my twenty-third birthday the year before last, I decided to pick up a pen . . .'

Loose Hands of Friendship

Simon Tasker

There are many ways in which a man can do his time.

There are those who choose to fight each day they face; bitterly battling with themselves, with inmates, taking on the screws and the system. Some decide to appeal their way through their sentence. Reading deep into the night they scrape through the small print of the law, challenging and questioning every detail of their case, searching like moles for holes, for precedents—a way through the gate. The erudite escape their empty hours by walking the avenue of education. They make up missing years by learning to read and write and then feverishly chase the classics around the library. Slowly moving on, they take up courses, exams, degrees, and, still slowly moving on, they think back and with a clever, wry smile remember the way they once thought.

Others look deep within themselves. And then look up to find God. With the main man in sight the hunt then turns to redemption. Another habit is to hit the gym and the weights. The challenge to change what's inside too much to face, they turn to what they can handle. Pumping iron replaces therapy and solid arms substitutes as a clean cut conscience.

There are far too many who live to get high. Too weak to stand up and fight for their existence they subjugate to temptation and escape under the hazy influences they covet, and the disassociating excuses that inevitably follow.

The nostalgic tend to cling tenaciously to the past. Refusing to let go of the man they have once been, they regale the receptive with the places they've been, what they've seen, what they've held, owned, consumed, while the desperately forlorn bombard girlfriends and wives with demanding letters, pestering phone calls and volatile visits.

Then there's the precious and solemn few who stand tall and stroll along the landings and their days in silence. With just their own strength of mind and character they achieve what every low-life inmate strives to create with easy alternatives; that is, their own isolated world in which they can safely breathe.

The day I looked down from the Fours landing and watched as Leigh first arrived on the wing, I'd have laid out two phone cards and a half ounce pouch (At least I would have if Santern hadn't been carted off the wing and down the block by the screws for running a Lottery syndicate) that he was one of the precious few.

I would have won too, if it hadn't have been for what went down.

I don't know what it was that made me so damned certain Leigh was going to walk straight and sure through his sentence with head held high. Maybe it was just the way he carried himself, or the way, at least to me, he seemed to be surrounded by an aura of dignity and self-possession. That he could stroll through dog shit and never even smell it.

With nothing much else to do but gossip I found out later on that same day that Leigh was serving a short and sweet sentence of just six months for some kind of corporate fraud. After observing how discreetly he made his way up the stairs to the Threes, and then privately eased the door to his cell shut as he unpacked his box of belongings, it came as no surprise.

Leigh was a soft-footed office boy if ever I saw one.

Now I was one of the select few who got as close to Leigh as he'd allow anyone to get. Being as private, insular and as secure within himself as he was, we formed what you'd call a real loose friendship, but a friendship based on a mutual obligation rather than any common interests we may have shared.

It took me nearly two years to get to the position I held within the prison when Leigh furtively approached me. When I initially arrived on the wing I spent the first three months establishing a rapport with both screws and inmates. It quickly got around I could be trusted on both sides, so after posting an application I had no problem getting taken on in the kitchen, one of the prime placements of employment in the whole of the prison.

Over the next year I worked my way up from sweeping floors to washing pots and pans to cleaning and pushing trolleys to veg prep to the number one spot of kitchen trustee. I now created the weekly menus, took care of stock control and rotation, cooked the officers' mess food, and, the point of it all, held the keys for the fridges and the pantries.

Within a month I was supplying the wing's half a dozen dedicated bodybuilders with fresh eggs, milk and cooked chicken, satiating the sweet-toothed with biscuits and cakes, delivering quarter pound bags of sugar and coffee to a dozen or so selected inmates, selling sandwiches at lunchtime for phonecards, smuggling out yeast three times a year for the brewery, preparing flasks of coffee for the Listeners, and, for the screws, unofficially organising individual meals and snacks. As a result my income rose to more than I could feasibly spend and I enjoyed numerous perks.

●   ●   ●

I was crashed out on my bunk in my pad, just tucking into a bacon and brown sauce with cheese sandwich I'd prepared and carried back from the kitchen, (You'll understand cholesterol's the least of my concerns) when there was a short and polite tap on my cell door. I stopped chewing and stared at the small spy hole for a moment. No-one, cons or screws, ever thinks to knock and then wait before entering.

'Yeah,' I said cautiously.

I was surprised to see Leigh's head pop round the door and ask if I could spare a moment. Intrigued, I waved him in.

As he stood at the end of the steel-framed bunk explaining what it was he wanted, I worked my way through breakfast, taking the opportunity to get a good look at him. Despite the fact he'd been on the wing a week it was the only second time I'd actually caught sight of Leigh. To be honest I'd forgotten he'd ever arrived. Watching him again though, I felt the same feelings as I did the day he originally graced the wing. That this was someone you couldn't touch, whose world was his alone. But, paradoxically, I can also clearly remember looking him up and down and thinking how much of an easy target he made.

Leigh's problem was there was nothing physical about him to keep the coyotes from snapping. He was tall but lean with a real soft complexion and wearing tortoise shell specs he kept absently pushing up the bridge of his nose. What made his image worse was the clumsy lump of Sellotape stuck right between his eyes that kept the frame intact.

The guy's unnatural pallor and the way he looked so pampered in such a grimy environment was another nail in his coffin. Watching Leigh reminded me of a time when I used to work way beyond these walls. . .

Every Friday afternoon the whole of the site I was labouring on would close down and the work force would gather at the mixer to collect their wages. Most of the time there'd be a hundred or so guys; all streaked with sweat and dirt, tired looking and rough, a week's stubble itching, faded denims, steel toe-capped boots.

Sooner or later the wages clerk would appear, walk across the yard with his briefcase and then call out names and hand out the pay packets. With mesmerised amusement and sweat-filled eyes I used to stand there and look across at the clerk in his clean black suit, his gelled hair, his pink softened skin, how his light clerical voice was almost drowned out by the cussing and coarseness, and I used to laugh out loud at the contrast.

Well that was how much Leigh stood out. I could feel the same kind of laugh coming on with noting the way his prison issue denims were immaculately worn and stiffly pressed, how his shoes were polished to a reflective shine, his soft, educated tone and passive manner. What really lit the neon sign swinging above his head and flashing 'Sitting Duck' though, was his hair.

Singing with condition and care, his curls and locks cascaded down his shoulders in a rolling effeminate tumble. It was immediately apparent how much time he consumed combing and brushing them and I reckoned he'd be spending most of his meagre wages on shampoo and mousse. To be perfectly candid, even when I got to know and like the guy, I'd still shake my head in bemusement at the cut. I mean, the dominant style for the majority of the cons was a practical and unremitting crew cut or going completely bald, and giving a shit about the way you looked on the wing anathema to most of them too.

Wiping bacon grease from off my chin I figured that the way Leigh stood he was heading for a whole heap of trouble. (I'd have collected on that bet too.)

●　　●　　●

It turned out the reason behind Leigh's visit was the fact that he was anaemic and he came to me because the pills the medical block prescribed him wouldn't help the shit shift from a cow's arse. What he wanted were a few good helpings of liver, maybe three times a week. Could I arrange it?

His question hanging, I thought it over. The meat itself was cheap enough, no problems in cooking it; when it was served to the population, the ungrateful fuckers generally ignored it, I couldn't see a problem.

So, on top of all the other little scams I had going and for the duration of Leigh's visit, every Monday, Wednesday and Friday I delivered to his cell a small tub of liver and gravy. Leigh reciprocated by passing my cell every canteen day and dropping off an ounce of GV's finest.

●　　●　　●

As time invariably does, it melts its way through days and weeks; slowly for some of us, at a crawl for others.

Over the following three months I discovered Leigh was one of those rare anomalies to be found in HMPs—a genuine bona fide silent type. In the process of delivering his iron-clad meals I'd attempt to engage him in small talk, but he never achieved higher than a C grade in conversation. What I also came to admire about the man was the way in which he kept to himself, never involving himself with the petty politics polluting the landings. I guess he decided that with his reserved nature and different social standing he'd be safer spinning out his short days alone. As a result Leigh quietly worked away on a computer course in the Ed' block and spent the rest of his time behind his door.

To my surprise and delight Leigh walked the wing in peace. After a couple of weeks I expected his troubles to begin, but they never did. As I've said, the man had a 'Kick Me' sign pinned high up on his back but why no one ever took up the offer was beyond me. I wondered if it could be down to how reticent he was and the way he discreetly isolated himself, but that seldom makes a difference. Perhaps he'd lined some heavy hitter's pocket and the word had got around. I just didn't know.

What I do know is that until half the population turned against him, Leigh glided through his days on a gently blowing breeze.

●　　●　　●

I was pleased at how much time had easily elapsed when Leigh revealed he was just two days away from walking tall and free through the main gate. It was a Monday evening, half an hour before bang up, and he was mopping the last spoonful of gravy up with a hunk of bread when he told me.

I can remember gazing at the photos pinned to the poster board above Leigh's head, glancing back down to his face and then feeling overwhelmed with a hot flowing liquid of jealous hatred and anger. With alarming surprise I found myself beginning to lean forward with the intention of grabbing hold of his hair and repeatedly slamming his head into the wall.

I wondered if it was a natural reaction to Leigh's imminent release, but the feeling transcended the traditional resentment. I think what hurt was the life Leigh was about to embrace. Through a combination of the photos of his house, his wife and kids, from the attractive suburban lifestyle he occasionally revealed in conversation, the manner in which he spoke and stood, his looks, his goddamned hair, I knew he was escaping not only this depraved shit hole, but he was escaping into a world I would never taste.

In that one moment of bitter clarity I understood his fear and appreciated why he remained so aloof.

I resisted striking out and instead observed the way Leigh characteristically wiped his mouth clean with tissue, carefully replaced the lid to the tub, and then obliviously offered me a ciggy. I lit up and felt the anger quickly dissipate.

We spent the next ten minutes discussing the plans he'd made for his first big day and as we did so it struck home I'd never again have the opportunity of transporting his tubs of liver and gravy. The irrevocable certainty of that fact whispered a great sadness within me.

After shaking Leigh's hand and wishing him luck, I returned to my own cell. For a while I just lay out on my bunk; pissed off and miserable, but unable to pin down exactly why I felt so deflated with Leigh's news, particularly in light of my initial, vitriolic reaction. I wondered if I'd let my guard slip and had grown attached enough to miss him being around, but it felt deeper than that.

As the screw banged the door shut for the last time that day, I thought maybe Leigh's presence had filled me with a little hope. Hope and a kind of tangible reminder that beyond the walls a decent life does exist, that there's more for every one of us than the putrescent mesh of hate and pain and fear and cruelty we're tangled up in.

With Leigh gone, I knew so too was that hope.

•   •   •

As it turned out I came into contact with Leigh for one final time, but under extremely different circumstances. As soon as I walked onto the wing during Tuesday evening's association period I felt the kinetic charge in the atmosphere. Warily ascending the stairs to the Fours and my pad, I experienced the same kind of premonitory pressure as I did when I was a kid.

Whenever I got hold of any balloons the first thing I'd always do was place a couple to the side to keep. I'd then proceed to happily blow up the rest until they'd burst. With the balloons getting bigger and bigger between my hands and in front of my face, it was expelling the last few lungfuls of air that had me hooked.

That same tense anticipation I felt in the few moments before the balloons popped, was the same feeling I had entering my pad; that something was about to go bang in front of my face, but I didn't know quite when.

I always keep two maxims in my head to guarantee that my world continues to safely revolve. One: don't get involved; the other: whatever it is, it's not my business. Only way to survive.

Rather than finding out what the hell was going on I stuck to my daily routine. After grabbing a towel, my wash-bag and some clean kit from my pad, I hit the showers.

•   •   •

I can't tell you how good it is to disappear. With the hot stream of water rhythmically falling, the embracing aroma of soap and shampoo, eyes closed, feeling relaxed, alone; I could've been anywhere. For twenty minutes my world was at peace but then, with the door swinging open and a cold draught of air penetrating my cocoon of warmth, the illusion collapsed.

I poked my head around the cubicle and was surprised to see the bulky, ripped up form of Laverton, the gym orderly and biggest fittest man in the nick, standing there. He normally used the showers over at the gym and so, respectfully nodding his way, I guessed he'd finished work early and never got the chance.

He nodded amiably back and then, stepping into an empty cubicle and speaking over the water, he just came right out with it.

'Look's like your mate's getting it tonight,' he said bluntly.

The atmosphere on the wing and the awareness it was Leigh's last night clicked like a locking gate.

'What's going on?' I asked, carefully keeping the edge out of my voice, but remembering the way I'd felt myself in Leigh's pad, the way I'd wanted to bounce his head of the wall.

'They'd planned on just boot polishing him up—you know the standard sending off?'

I nodded with understanding. Being smeared with boot polish, possibly having your eyebrows removed and being roughed up a bit was the traditional way the wing waved goodbye.

'But Buckton came up with the 'better' idea of dragging him into the TV room and shaving off all his hair, stripping him and then lobbing him out onto the landing.' Laverton said.

I immediately pictured an image of Leigh quietly reading in his pad, just a few hours away from freedom, and then the shock and fright on his face as his pad door swings violently open and he's rushed by a dozen inmates, dragged along the landing, his glasses deliberately smashed, his terror and feeling of complete indignation, with the awakening realisation of what it is they're exactly going to do, the angry buzzing as the shears close in, the echoes of tormenting laughter, futile, painful struggles, tears squeezed shut . . . .

Consumed with a silent rage I stepped out of the shower, snatched my towel of the wall peg and began to dry myself down. 1 could sense Laverton impassively watching, and waving away the usual caution I reserved, I looked him straight in the eye. 'And you don't think it's in any way out of order?' I demanded.

'Nothing to do with me,' he replied. 'And he's done nothing for me. No skin off my nose either way.'

I slipped into some blue, prison issue shorts and then perched on the wooden bench to pull on my socks.

'Look,' I said, 'if Leigh had immersed himself in the bullshit that goes on out there, if he'd in any way brought this on himself, I wouldn't give a shit, but the bloke's not said a word since he's been on the wing. Not one fucking word.'

Laverton shrugged.

'Maybe he should have. Maybe if he'd made the effort; maybe if he'd cut his hair, neglected to iron his denims now and again and didn't wander around like some goddamned superior peacock faggot, he wouldn't have got so many people's backs up.'

'That's not what this is about.' I snapped back. 'That's not what this is about at all. He's an easy target and Buckton and whoever else joins in are just taking advantage of that fact. If you decided to grow your hair long and never leave your pad, do you think they'd come after you? Not a chance and you know it.'

'You're right,' said Laverton, 'they probably wouldn't, but do you really believe that if I was talking to that pale faggot now and it was you stood in his shoes, he'd give a shit about you? He'd let you fry without giving it a second thought,'

'That's not the point.' I said.

'Not, the point,' Laverton interjected, 'is that you're showing concern for the wrong fool. You're on a good screw here—you don't wanna fuck it up. Besides,' he reasoned, 'Leigh's a big boy, he's getting released tomorrow—so fuck him. Let him take care of himself.'

I pushed on my shoes watching Laverton rub shampoo into his hair and as the lather thickly foamed, I tried again.

'It'll destroy him,' I stated. Laverton ignored me and spread the lather over his chest. I tried to elaborate. 'To do something like that to someone like Leigh would be the same as banning you from ever using the gym again, or taking away my kitchen job, or . . . '

'Jesus,' insisted Laverton, 'he's only getting a haircut.'

'Yeah, I know that, but it goes beyond that. To Leigh, his appearance, his hair is who he is. To fuck with that aspect of him is to fuck about with something inside of him. I don't know what, his pride, his dignity, something deeper maybe. Whatever it is, I just know it's wrong.' Laverton shrugged dismissively again, turned his back and soaked his face under the water. I finished dressing and then just stood for a moment, Leigh's face flashing across my mind as they pin him down and close in with the shears.

Laverton turned back round and seemed surprised to still see me standing there.

'You've been steaming the veg for too long man,' he said roughly, stepping out of the shower and grabbing his own towel. 'Gone to your fucking head.'

'It's just wrong.' I insisted.

Laverton stared hard for a moment and then shaking his head disparagingly, warned me, 'You never heard any of this from me. They're gonna rush him ten minutes before bang up when the screws are counting the 'tools' in, so you've got enough time to warn Leigh to either get himself off the wing or bang himself up early. You're taking a big risk though,' he added. 'I hope you understand that. They're gonna know it was you.'

I nodded.

'Fair enough,' he said, 'Respect you for that. But what you've also got to remember is that long after Leigh's gone and forgotten, you'll still be here. If I was you I'd let it go.' He leant down and grabbing his toiletries and pulling open the door, he advised me to think about it.

●   ●   ●

Heading swiftly to my pad it wasn't until I'd spotted my familiar kitchen whites slung over the back of the chair that I was slapped hard in the face with doubt. Standing rooted to the spot in the centre of my cell I stared through the uniform as it seemed to epitomise everything I was about to sacrifice, including all the time it had taken to get to where I was. A cold part of me began to question exactly what intended to do and I asked myself was it really worth it? After all, it was only a haircut they were planning, it would grow back, no point alienating myself for someone who was walking large and free. And anyway, maybe Laverton was right, and Buckton's behaviour was completely justified. And even if it turned out they were wrong, if the forthcoming attack on Leigh was out of order, who was I to step in and intervene? Leigh's Dark Knight?

The fact of the matter was I owed Leigh nothing. The only connection between us was the loose hands of friendship, but a friendship based on a mutual understanding. Nothing more than that.

I smiled thinly with longing at the temptation of just ignoring Leigh's troubles and sitting it out. Realising my intentions of doing an exact antithesis to what common sense sagely advised, the cold voice boiled over into outrage. 'Fuck him,' it ordered, 'be a hard-arse and turn away.' But that was something I simply couldn't do. Pulling open the cell door, I stepped out onto the landing.

Moving towards Leigh's pad I knew if I had decided not to step in and offer Leigh my hand, then I'd walk from that point on with an even longer shadow than Buckton. It would mean I'd sunk as deep as this place. As far as I'm concerned no matter where you are, however shite your surroundings, you go on and do what you know is right. Go any other way and you're selling yourself short and using your present circumstances, no matter how depraved they may be, as a rather diluted excuse.

Truth of the matter was; Leigh was a friend. Or about as good a friend as you can make in here. What I'd done was question the value and meaning of that friendship so I could drain away the responsibility I felt.

I wasn't that much of an arsehole to take it all the way though.

•   •   •

Ignored by the heavy presence of inmates littering the landings, I cautiously approached Leigh's cell, but as soon as I turned to his door I felt the population's attention snap my way. A thick curtain of silence suddenly fell and I knew if I turned around and fronted their scrutiny, I'd probably bottle it.

Knocking quickly on Leigh's door I pushed forward but found it locked. Breathing a sigh of relief I lifted the latch covering the spy hole to tell Leigh to keep himself locked in, and then closed my eyes in dismay. The cell was empty.

I spun round, mentally listing all possibilities of where he could be, and then there he was, just stepping out of the recess at the end of the landing.

After acknowledging my presence with a wave he made his way towards me. Concentrating on Leigh I heard and felt a collective movement above and below me, and sensing there wasn't much time, yelled at Leigh to hurry the fuck up. With a puzzled frown he looked along the landing, pausing in mid step, and then I screamed at him to run as the door five cells behind him swung open ejecting an ambush party comprising Buckton and three of his mates.

At the same time I heard the crashing of running footsteps on the metal grille of the landing, emanating from the staircase, and realised we were being surrounded and ultimately trapped. There was nowhere to escape but into Leigh's pad.

I looked on helplessly as Leigh, in almost infuriatingly slow-mo fashion, turned around. Spotting Buckton closing, he abruptly awoke to the imminent danger he was in, and finally punching the fast forward button began racing towards me.

As he ran, he pulled the key to his pad from his pocket and hurled it my way. Catching it on the bounce and praying the door wasn't double-locked, I slid in the key and turned it, began to push open the door thinking we'd made it, then an arm clamped around my neck and tried dragging me to the floor.

Choking for air I forced myself backwards and slammed my assailant into the landing railings. I heard the wind knock out of him but he clung on, and then bodies swarmed over me. With my arms and legs pinned I flicked my head to the side and with a certain amount of pride and respect watched Leigh vainly battling it out. After a moment of struggling violently someone grabbed him from behind and locked him in a 'sleeper'. With his airway cut off the fight was over.

I turned my attention to Buckton and despite the situation almost broke out in laughter. With his shiny bald head, the scruffy gym vest stretched over his fat stodgy gut, the cartoon of tattoos colouring his arms, his rotten teeth and nicotine stained fingers he exaggerated every stereotype underlined in the convicts guide to survival.

He scowled at my smirk. 'Who the fuck invited you to the party?' he said.

'Just leave him alone.' I answered.

Ignoring me, Buckton asked, 'What I'd like to know is why the interest?' He sneered and looking around him said, 'You're not sharing beds the pair of you? I mean, if that's the case, if it's love were talking about, then I understand and wouldn't want to get in the way, but if not...' He raised his hands expansively.

Over the sycophantic sniggers I told him to go fuck himself. He took a step towards me. 'Piss off.' he said, menacingly, 'Mind your own business and piss off otherwise you're gonna spoil our little party.' He nodded across and the hands around my neck and pinning me down released their hold. I glanced at Leigh who couldn't bear to look at me, and then I turned back to Buckton. 'I'm not walking away.' I said.

'Back off!' he growled. 'I won't tell you again.'

I panned helplessly around and shook my head in disgust and disappointment at the amount of people standing atavistically watching, and the fact that several inmates I sorted out with extra food were involved. It also struck me how easily insignificant pricks who never spoke up for themselves and people who should no better all gelled together. All it had taken was an easy target and a leader.

'Let's get this hippie into the recess,' Buckton instructed and as they began to drag Leigh off I leapt forward. Buckton whipped round punching me clean and hard in the jaw and I fell back and lay stunned for a moment.

'You shouldn't have done that motherfucker! '

The threat curdling violence held in the voice broke through my daze and I half sat up to turn towards its source. I almost sang for joy seeing Laverton peering down from the Fours landing, his expression asking me what did I tell you and aren't you the biggest arsehole under the sun. Focusing back on Buckton he said, 'That man you just put down happens to be a friend of mine.'

Buckton glanced quickly across at me wishing I'd disappear, and then looked back up at Laverton and swallowing nervously, nodded an apology. Buckton was big, but he had nothing else and he knew it.

'We were just sending someone off,' he said meekly. 'Which was fine until you stepped over the line,' said Laverton. 'Now it either ends or we take it all the way.'

Buckton shrugged indifferently. 'Makes no difference to me,' he said. 'Good.' said Laverton, 'We'll call it a night then.'

I stepped out of the way as Buckton walked off towards the stairs, and sardonically noted how quickly everyone else involved had slipped into the shadows once the odds had evened out a bit.

'You alright?' Laverton asked me.

'I'm fine,' I said gratefully. 'Thanks for stepping in.' I added.

'No problem, you just keep those eggs and chicken coming.'

I smiled at his sarcasm. Rubbing his neck Leigh turned to Laverton and began to offer his gratitude, but Laverton stopped him dead.

'It wasn't for you,' he said abruptly. 'As far as I'm concerned they could have left you hanging off the safety netting. The only reason behind what I did was that man stood there.'

I looked up at Laverton and didn't believe what he'd just said for a minute.

I stood watching him as he walked away and thought about how he'd just happened to catch me in the showers at the right time. Took me another two seconds to twig on that maybe what Laverton had said standing under the water in the showers was deliberate. I called out and he turned around.

'Yeah,' he said.

I studied him for a moment and then answered, 'Doesn't matter' and I let the man get on his way.

Loose Hands of Friendship © Simon Tasker 2000

The main character of this story has no redeeming features. It was written in HMP Kingston as an exercise given by the prison's writer-in-residence. **Ian P. Downes**, the writer, says 'I accept this is very violent and thick with bad attitude, the whole point is get over just how some people really think.'

One Friend Only

Ian P. Downes

Your round Dave, mine's another pint.

Isn't it time you headed home to your wife Simon?

Nah, with the way things are with her at the moment, I'd sooner stay out.

I thought you two were safe together after all these years mate? So what's the problem?

She found a phone number in my jacket and it was this bird Sandra from work. Anyway, she phoned her and found out we'd been having it off for the last six months. Now the bitch wants a divorce and that means my car will have to go.

Shit, that's heavy stuff mate, but won't she change her mind? Buy her some flowers, and take her out for a meal or some thing.

I already got her some flowers, and she belted me over the head with them. The bastards cost me three quid as well!

So what about the kids, you know she'll screw you for maintenance now, don't you? A mate of mine has to pay a hundred notes a week for his two, thanks to the C.S.A.

Bastard C.S.A.: screw every one. Bastard kids as well, I only put her up the club because she wanted them. I'd sooner have my car than those screaming brats.

Yeah, well I'd better piss off home to my missus or I'll be in shit as well. See ya Simon.

Yeah, see ya Dave, and if your old woman nags ya just tell her to go screw herself.

Simon slowly walked back through the dirty streets of Dagenham. Work all day at the car plant and when you get home your old woman fucking nags ya. Well balls to you, you old tart, I've got my car and I'll soon pick up another old tart.

Arriving home, he finds the house empty and his first thought is that she's left him and taken his car. So rushing out to the garage he bangs open the door. His bright red XR3i is still where he left it.

Hello Baby, Daddy's home, he says, as he gently strokes the gleaming bodywork. Opening the door and getting inside, he sits and strokes the steering wheel until he falls asleep.

The next morning he's woken from his sleep by his wife shaking his shoulder. Simon, Simon, it's time you left for work. Here, drink this tea.

Waking up, Simon sees his wife holding a mug of tea out towards him. Not in the car you silly cow, he shouts, you might spill it.

His wife puts the tea on the garage floor and walks out of the garage.

Stupid cow, she may have spilt it in you baby, he says stroking the steering wheel. Still mumbling to himself, he gets out of the car and gently closes the door, before picking up the tea and walking out of the garage.

Where were you last night, he asks his wife?

I went to see a friend, she says and as the children were sleepy they stayed the night there. I'm going to collect them later and take them to school.

Thought it was a bit too fucking quiet round here, he says. Anyway I thought you were leaving and divorcing me?

Do you really want that Simon? asks his wife.

You do what ya want girl. Me, I'm going to work and just make sure my dinner's on the table tonight when I get in.

I don't think I'll be in until later, his wife says, because I'm going up town to do a bit of shopping.

Just make sure you spend your own money, and if you don't have my grub ready when I get in, then don't come back at all. Going out he slams the front door shut.

The hooter goes, and the first team leaves the production lines for their tea break. Simon walks into the canteen, gets a mug of tea and a bacon roll and goes over to where Dave is sitting.

Hiya mate, says Dave. I waited for you this morning, but you didn't turn up.

Nah, the old woman gave me a hard time and I was late, so I caught a bus in.

You look like shit Simon, and you ain't even changed your clothes yet from last night. The bitch has stopped washing my stuff now, so I'll have to do some later on. Shit, things are really bad then?

For sure, the cow only had the balls to say she was going up town shopping today, but I soon put a stop to that. I told her, if my grub ain't on the table when I get in, then I'll slap her. You should have seen her crawl then.

So you really think she'll leave you then?

Yeah, perhaps, but if she does, then I'll just get another bird to move in. Maybe I'll even let Sandra move in. At least she hasn't got any kids to bother me, and she's a great screw, gives a hell of a blow-job.

Yeah well you could be right, but your Paula is a nice looking woman. Where's Sandra anyway, normally she's behind the counter doing teas.

I asked, but she phoned in sick today. Probably still getting over our last shag, laughed Simon.

Just then the hooter went again and it was time to get back to the production line once more. For the rest of that shift Simon worked on the line and grumbled about his wife to himself.

After work, he went straight to the pub and drank the night away. At closing time, he went to a phone box and phoned Sandra. The phone rang and rang, and he was just about to hang up when Sandra answered.

Hello, she said. Hiya lover, how about I come round and we spend some time together in bed? Simon said.

Sorry Simon, but I've got one of my girlfriends round at the moment and anyway I'm not feeling very well.

They said at work that you'd phoned in sick, and I thought you were still sore after our last session together.

Just then he heard a giggle in the background and heard Sandra shushing some one. What's going on there, he asked?

It's just my friend looking through some old photos of mine, that's all.

So when can I come round then and have a shag? You know you like the old trouser snake, don't you?

Look Simon, I've got to go. I'll see you at work in a few days and we can sort something out then, alright?

Yeah right, he said as he dumped the receiver back onto the phone cradle. Fucking women, never there when you want them, and when they are there, they only fucking nag.

Stumbling through the night, Simon arrived home to find an empty house and no dinner. Still grumbling to himself, he went to the garage and sat in his car stroking the steering wheel and talking to it until he fell asleep.

Later that night he woke up with a splitting headache and went to find an aspirin. As he banged the kitchen door open he heard a noise upstairs. So, turning round he climbed the stairs and went into the bedroom, where his wife was in bed.

You fucking bitch, he screamed. Where was my dinner when I got in? It's your fucking fault that I've got a headache now.

He then punched his wife in the face, as she was sitting up, splitting her lip and knocking her out cold.

The children had woken up with all the noise and the six year old was crying. So banging into the children's room, he shouted. Shut the fuck up you little bastards or I'll belt you. The six year old was too scared to stop crying. So grabbing hold of him, Simon shook him and threw him back onto the bed. The ten year old just laid there with wide scared eyes.

Slamming the bedroom door behind him, Simon went to the bathroom and ripped open the medicine cabinet and swept the contents on the floor until he found the aspirin. Swallowing four, he went back to the garage, got in his car and fell asleep.

The next morning he woke up and went to the kitchen. His wife was there and her mouth was swollen badly. The children cowered away from him and kept their heads down, hoping he wouldn't see them.

Let that be a lesson, bitch. Tonight you have my dinner ready or you'll get another one. With that he slammed out of the house and went to meet Dave for his lift to work

All day Simon was on a high because he had really taught the bitch a lesson and knew that from now on she'd be too scared not to do anything he wanted. He wished he'd done it before because women were only good for shagging, cleaning and cooking anyway. He didn't even mind too much that Sandra was still off work

That night after his shift ended, he went to the pub again and as the night wore on, he got drinking with a woman in her forties. Closing time came round and the landlord called time. Simon and his new lady friend staggered out into the night holding onto each other. Wanna come back to my place? asked the woman, in a drunken slur.

Yeah, why not, he said.

So off they went, staggering into the night and falling over together.

At the woman's flat they undressed and fell into bed. Simon couldn't get an erection so he blamed her and swore at her. Fucking woman, get a bloke drunk and blame him when he can't get it up.

But the woman wasn't listening. She'd fallen asleep with her mouth open. So laying back on the bed, Simon fell asleep thinking of his red car.

The next morning he again woke with a splitting headache, and stumbling out of the strange bed, he caught his foot in his clothes and fell, banging his head on the wall. Bastard, bastard, bastard he shouted still laying on the floor and watching the room revolve, as he rubbed his aching head.

The woman woke up and, seeing him like this, she started to laugh.

This was too much for him and he flew into a rage. Getting off the floor he jumped onto the bed and punched that laughing face. It felt good so he kept on punching it until the screams stopped and red blood covered everything.

I must polish my car tonight, he thought, as he looked down at the pulped face below him. This made him laugh and while laughing he started to urinate. So holding onto himself, he directed the stream of urine over the smashed face below him.

That's all women are any good for, he said, pissing on. He climbed off the bed, got dressed and left for work.

At tea break, Dave sniffed as he sat down at the table. You're getting a bit high aint ya mate?

I hadn't noticed, said Simon, but I'll have a bath later . . . maybe.

What's all that on your jacket, Dave asked?

Looking down, Simon saw dried puke on his jacket and trousers. Yeah, well I had a bit too many last night, picked up this young bird about nineteen and we spent the night screwing.

What about Paula bet she wasn't too happy, was she?

Couldn't give a fuck, anyway didn't go home. We spent the night shagging and I even gave her a good going over before leaving this morning. This made him laugh, because he remembered her face and the blood all over the place.

For the rest of his shift Simon thought about the great night he'd had and decided to do it again tonight. He knew a few pubs where the slags went so it would be easy for him to pick up another one.

As he was clocking off Dave came up to him.

Look mate, I know you're having problems at home and Paula won't do your stuff for you. Well why not put some in a bag and I'll ask my missus to do it?

Yeah sure, but I'm alright now and the bitch will either do it, or I'll slap her. Anyway, why the sudden concern about how I look?

It's not just that, Simon, you stink a bit as well and . . .

Look, you can fuck off if that's what you think. Anyway I've just done a days graft and I ain't into no fucking beauty contest. So if all you're gonna do is slag me off you can go fuck yourself.

Simon then stamped off to the bus stop mumbling to himself.

Last orders found Simon drunk in his local. He hadn't managed to pick up a woman and was in a bad mood, his head hurt and he felt cold. Leaving the pub, he found it was raining and by the time he arrived home he was wet and very angry. Throwing open the front door, he stumbled inside.

Where's my fucking grub, you fucking whore he shouted but there was no reply. The house was empty.

He climbed the stairs and ripped all Paula's clothes from the closet and threw them down the stairs. He then went into the children's room and did the same with their clothes and toys. He then took them into the back garden piled them in a heap and tried to set them alight. However they wouldn't burn very well because of the rain. His head was hurting even more, so he gave up and went back inside. Walking into the garage he stood and looked at his car.

Hello my beautiful darling, Daddy's back again, he said, as he lovingly stroked the wing. Fuck I'm wet, but I can't sit in you like this, can I baby?

So he stripped off his clothes and threw them on the garage floor.

There he sat stroking the steering wheel and shivering I'm going to turn you on baby and you'll soon warm me up. So he started the car and put the heater on full. Once the engine had warmed up he revved it and because it sounded so lovely he revved it again. Without realising it, he had gained an erection.

I love you my beautiful baby, he said, stroking the steering wheel. Why can't women be like you?

He started to nod off to sleep and was soon snoring peacefully.

Shortly after this, Paula came back home. Seeing the mess, she knew Simon was home and expected him to come and hit her again. So being as quiet as she could she went round the house trying to gather some clothes for her and the children. Following the trail she saw them piled in the garden.

Oh you bastard, she said, why have you changed like this? Well now you've gone too far, I'm taking the kids away for good.

As she stood there, she heard the sound of an engine running. So walking to the garage, she carefully looked in. As she opened the door, the carbon monoxide fumes hit her. Seeing Simon sitting behind the steering wheel, she silently shut the door again.

I hope your car takes you straight to hell, she said as she walked out of the front door.

One Friend Only © Ian P. Downes 2000

Paul S. Agutter of HMP Glenochil, Scotland is a former university lecturer whose two stories in earlier issues of *Prison Writing*, were about an unemployed minotaur and corporate exploitation in Africa. *The Fur Coat*, which he describes as 'a lightweight piece', is further evidence of his growing reputation as a writer.

The Fur Coat

Paul S. Agutter

It was a distinguished art critic and historian familiar to BBC audiences and readers of Sunday broadsheets who ensured the early success of Angus MacGillivray. Thousands visiting the painter's second London exhibition parroted the critic's rhapsodies on the spare yet transcendent descriptions of the commonplace wrought by this new and *original* talent. Strikingly tall, saturnine and remote, the artist's person synergized with this sudden fame. Tentative commissions were mostly refused with an abruptness wholly in character.

Julie's father was a long-standing friend of the distinguished critic and over sherry and hors d'oeuvres, Julie learned about the glittering career that stretched before MacGillivray's feet. 'Look at that huge oil of Handa Island. Utterly compelling. The vast age of those dark red cliffs, the splintered textures of the pinnacles, the inimical otherness of the breakers, the soaring hunger of the sea-birds . . . ' Julie noted that MacGillivray would be attending the gallery in person again in two days' time. Dressed to maim if not quite to kill, she arrived shortly after the doors were opened and stationed herself before the Handa Island canvas. Her pose was perfect. Her shoes pinched slightly.

'I can sense the vast age of those dark red cliffs,' she murmured, aware at last of a tall figure detaching itself from a nearby cloud of sycophants. 'The texture of those splintered pinnacles, the inimical otherness of the breakers, the soaring hunger of the birds.'

'Romantic?' he sneered.

Quickly, she shook her head.

'Not so . . . contrived. More precise. More . . . alien.'

'Like a photograph, perhaps?'

'Nonsense,' she snapped. Then she glanced round at him and allowed her face to flood with embarrassed recognition. He smiled a calculatedly wicked smile. He studied her face and his long fingers curled.

'You know Handa?' he inquired; pleasantly enough.

'As well as anyone can, thank you,' she muttered, 'though I've never been there.' Then with exquisite timing she floated away towards the exit. She paused near the doors to look back at him, studiously enigmatic, framed in blonde; and was gone. Three months later, they were married.

It was a success. Thanks to the contacts he made through Julie's family, MacGillivray's commissions grew steadily more lucrative. His income enabled Julie to live in the style that her hard-pressed father had been unable to support. Friends remarked that marriage had both tamed and liberated her. Her fidelity to her husband surprised the less discerning, for her youth had been of the kind honoured less in sonnets than in limericks. But if she had once been accounted cheap, she was beyond doubt expensive, and she was not prepared to risk her Knightsbridge apartment or her Cotswold retreat. Of course there were whispers about the handsome young disciple of MacGillivray who seemed to idolise the artist's wife more than the artist, but there are always whispers. An admirer need not be a lover; money might grant one liberty without making one a libertine. And all the best people were to be found at those social gatherings where Julie was a swirl of satin and laughter, jewels glittering like seabirds' eyes, her husband a silent presence beside the door.

Her personality expanded with her wardrobe. Elegant in ball gown, managerial in business suit, playful in denim, lethal in fur, Julie was one with her clothes. The more MacGillivray's paintings sold, the more outfits she purchased and the more the hidden dimensions of her character emerged. Whether her husband relished or resented this deployment of the rewards of his creativity, none could say. He seemed, in his brooding way, to bask in her social glory; but while his talent grew no less, his work darkened. Its studies of wild creatures became suffused with the sorrows of mortality. He would skin and dissect his subjects to reveal their secret depths.

He was seldom commissioned for portraits.

But he was commissioned to paint a new altarpiece for a church in northern Norway. He was not known for religious paintings, but the small Catholic community in that staunchly Protestant land had offered sixty thousand kroner plus expenses to an established artist willing to undertake the task; there was probably support from the Vatican. MacGillivray accepted. He spent a long summer in Norway while Julie stayed in London or in their Cotswold village, the admiring disciple in regular attendance.

MacGillivray wandered around the summer tundra or sat above the vast cliffs, letting the sealight and the flux of sub-Arctic life flow through his eyes, his fingers curling around imagined brush or charcoal. Through the long hours of undarkness he sketched, painted, dissected. He studied and planned, refining and rejecting, tireless and silent. And before the long nights and the bitter snows returned he had adorned the church's east wall with a Madonna and Child in Norwegian garb, set against rock and sea and surrounded by the living creatures of the far north. If the darkness of his recent work was there it was well hidden.

The people thanked him; he was praised by a cardinal. The distinguished critic chartered a flight to visit the new work, at BBC expense, and declared it a masterpiece.

MacGillivray returned home with a new reputation as a religious artist, sixty thousand kroner, and a gift for his wife.

'I want to take you there before this winter, my love,' he urged.

'I'd love to go, but it's such a long way and Diana absolutely insists we're here for her evening a week on . . .'

'Just a short visit. We needn't stay. But it's important to me. We met there, yet you've never been.'

She laughed lightly.

'Oh, darling . . . But why now?'

'It was Norway. It reminded me . . . I was homesick. The urge to return . . .

She yielded with a good grace, as one must in the interests of harmony and profit, and three mornings later they alighted on the sloping eastern shore of Handa Island, two of a dozen late-season tourists on the little boat. Scolded by skuas, surrounded by binoculars and cameras and anoraks, they set off along the path that climbed westwards towards those massive Pre-Cambrian cliffs that his brush had immortalised so many years before.

'Angus, dear, what *have* you got in that huge pack?' she demanded for the twentieth time.

'Curiosity?'

'Quite safe. I'm not a cat.'

'Sure?'

'*Perfectly* sure.'

'A little further, then . . . Listen—you can hear the breakers! Razorbills, puffins, skuas . . . Can you smell it?'

'Yes, Angus. Now don't tease me any longer. What . . . ?'

He unfastened the pack and drew out her gift.

'Why—Angus! Oh, darling, you shouldn't have! I've got two fur coats already! But this is—this is..'

'Different?'

'It's beautiful!'

'Good. Put it on.'

'Here? But darling, it's hardly appropriate . . . '

'The wind's chilly, my dear. You have goose bumps.'

'That's just excitement. Oh, very well. Just for a moment, though, or everyone will stare.'

'I know they will.'

The fur settled softly around her body and a strange light grew in her eyes. Without a word she broke from him and rushed away into the wind's teeth, towards the edge of the great cliff. He called her name but her step never faltered. In a moment she was gone. There were screams from their fellow-passengers and perhaps the interminable cries of the birds were for an instant harsher; but the agony of the splintering breakers a 150 metres below was undiminished.

The inquiry into Julie's bizarre accident, or suicide, took many ponderous weeks. Her innumerable friends offered guarded condolences. MacGillivray bore it all stoically. When it was over the officer in charge of the investigation went for a drink with the bereaved artist. He was sympathetic, but something troubled him.

'That fur coat, Mr MacGillivray. I hope you won't mind my asking . .

'Yes?'

'We had it examined by experts, you see.'

'And?'

'Well, sir . . . They said it wasn't mink, or mole, or beaver—in fact they couldn't work out what it was, though they said it was definitely real.'

'Oh, yes. It's real.'

'Do you happen to know, sir? What animal the fur came from?'

'Yes. I know.'

'So, would you mind . . . ?'

But the artist's eyes were focused on a place far beyond the officer's shoulder, on the wild unyielding cliffs of the distant north.

'Lemming,' he confessed.

The Fur Coat © Paul S. Agutter 2000

Michael Grant is an inmate of HMP Ford, Sussex. Aged 30, he was drawn to writing for many years but it was only when he was sent to prison that he began a course that got him started. This is one of his first short stories.

When Wishes Come True

Michael Grant

Shadows thrown by the moon fall like ghostly apparitions across the ground. The ground is covered by a frost that reflects the obscure light, making it appear as if thousands of tiny diamonds have been scattered upon it. There is a sinister silence floating through the air, leaving George Philips with nothing to listen to. With his head bent low into the collars of his jacket, he eases his glasses back up his nose and quickens his step. He starts to wish he wasn't reading the novel *Keepers of the Maze* about a group of fanatics who believe it is their calling in life to keep the population of New York down to a manageable level. And how they did it wasn't an issue, just so long as it's gruesome. During the summer, after his nightshift at the sorting office, walking through the park was a pleasant stroll, but at this time of year, just before Christmas, it was creepy.

The hairs on George's neck stiffen as he senses he isn't alone. He stops still, simultaneously removing his hands from his coat pockets. With his feet firmly placed shoulders width apart he scans the park near and far. His breathing changes to short rapid, oxygen-conserving gasps. Over to his right, in a cluster of bushes, something moves. George's eyes zero in on the target. He sees nothing suspicious. His ears follow suit, maybe a slight echo of movement, he can't be sure. His nose, the only other sense with long range capabilities, scrutinises the area. However, George's brain, the general in this little battle, decides not to wait for this reconnaissance report. It orders George to retreat; on the double!

He turns and starts running. For a short man he's taking long bounding strides. He reaches an incredible speed, unfortunately it is too fast for the slippery frost. George loses his footing as he tries to negotiate a tight bend that steers around a pond. And he skids face down and head first into some bushes. Scrambling to his feet and ignoring his missing glasses, he sees a dark shape moving towards him. George takes off again, too scared to think what it could be. He covers the thousand metres back to the sorting office in world record time.

• • •

The Christmas tree is small and made of shiny green plastic, the lights decorating it flash through the colours of the rainbow, making the silver dress of the fairy perched on the tree's summit appear to randomly change colour. Louise is smiling a beaming smile of content, as she watches her only child open her presents. First the little ones that just over a week ago were destined to be the only ones. She looks on as eleven-year-old Lisa rips the paper from her new shoes and gloves. Lisa mixes thanking her mother with the excited rush of putting on the gifts. Her long black hair, back into a pony tail, swishes from side to side as she runs around the room, clapping her hands, making dull sounds with the gloves. She runs at her mother and jumps into her lap and hugs her.

'Thanks Mummy!' she shouts.

'You're sure they're ok?' asks Louise.

'Yes mummy, they're just like the ones all my friends are wearing.'

Louise gazes into her eyes. They're bright and blue and reflecting the lights from the Christmas tree as much as the fairy's dress. She seems truly happy with her presents. Louise thinks how lucky she is to have such a beautiful child, one so well adjusted, so unaffected by the peer pressures that push other kids towards material things. There is only one thing that Lisa wants, and Louise wished so much that Paul could be there to see her finally get it. She could see so much of Paul in Lisa, his sparkling blue eyes, his small nose and his jet-black hair, and his complete enjoyment of life, just for life's sake, nothing else.

'What's wrong mummy?' Louise hadn't noticed the tears welling in her eyes.

'Nothing sweetheart, I was just thinking about Daddy.'

'You said Daddy's with us mummy, he's watching us now, making sure we're ok. He went to sleep before the car crashed and now he's watching us in his sleep.'

The tears spill from Louise's eyes. She rubs her cheek against Lisa's, savouring the feeling of soft skin next to soft skin.

'I know darling . . . ' she pauses, kissing Lisa on the cheek, 'there's another present for you under my bed.' Lisa jumps off her mother's lap and heads for the door.

'Lisa.' Lisa stops and looks at her mother.

'Yes mummy?' she says, with excitement edging her towards the door.

'You said that if you ever got one,' Louise places her hands in front of her mouth trying to hold back the mixture of joy and tears.

'Yes mummy?'

Louise removes her hands and quietly whispers, 'You'd be the best by the time you were eighteen!' Lisa stiffens with shock and surprise.

'Go my sweet darling, go and be the best!'

For a few seconds Lisa seems unable to move, then in an instant she is gone, with the sound of her new shoes on the stairs, trying its best to keep up with her. With peardrop tears falling from her cheeks, Louise looks up to the heavens and thanks God from the bottom of her heart.

•   •   •

George wakes up feeling the sunshine on his face, he hears noises coming from the kitchen and instantly feels like a cup of tea.

'We've been invited to the Royal Albert Hall next Saturday, there's a car coming to pick us up.' George looks at his wife as if she has just spoken in a foreign language.

'What're you talking about now?' he asks, trying to stifle a yawn.

Handing him an expensive looking envelope she says, 'here look for yourself' George takes the envelope and pulls out its contents.

> Mr. and Mrs. Philips
> Please accept this invitation
> To the Royal Albert Hall
> On Saturday 12th June 2000 at 8.00 p.m.
> For a special concert in your honour
> Please ring the following number to confirm.

George read the number and instantly assumed it was some kind of trick to get people on the phone. So that they could sell you double-glazing, as you paid for the phone bill. 'It's some kind of sales gimmick!' he said, while throwing the invite onto the kitchen table.

'Well it's a good gimmick,' responded his wife, 'because they're sending us a car and we've got front row seats.'

George looks at her in amazement. 'How do you know that?'

'I rang the number first thing, I wasn't going to miss any kind of chance to go to the Royal Albert Hall.' She looked excited as she poured him a cup of tea.

'So it's real then?' George's mind was trying to work out who would play such a trick on them, but he couldn't think of anyone. His wife's excitement began to rub off on him. 'The Royal Albert Hall, front row seats. I'll need a new suit!'

'I bought you one this morning,' she said, smiling.

George spent the following week telling all his colleagues that he was going to a concert at the Royal Albert Hall and that he had front row seats. He spent all Saturday afternoon on the phone telling all his relatives, after his wife checked to see if there would be anything on the telly worth recording and she realised that the concert was going to be televised live. They were both checking for the tenth time whether or not the video was set correctly when the doorbell rang. George opened the door to a man who was wearing a full chauffeur's uniform including the hat. George smiled and offered him his hand but was unable to shake it when he looked past the man and spotted the shiny black limousine parked in the middle of the road. All the neighbours were outside looking at it and their kids were trying to look through the blacked-out windows.

'We won't be a minute mate,' said George finally managing to shake the man's hand. Once inside the limousine the chauffeur told them there was champagne in the cooler and a telephone between the seats if they wanted to make a call, George and his wife looked at each other. After a couple of glasses of champagne and just a few quick calls to the kids and grandchildren to make sure they'd be watching. George realised that in the excitement they hadn't bothered to check who had sent the invite and why, but when he asked the chauffeur he answered that he wasn't obliged to say.

The red carpet and all the photographers felt great but standing in the VIP bar with all these celebrities was something else. His wife kept nudging him every time someone famous walked passed, at this rate thought George he would have a sore arm by the time the night was over.

George listened to and enjoyed all the music he heard. He had always liked classical music and even had a CD or two but had never experienced it live. He was amazed at how good it sounded and made a mental note to save up for one of those expensive stereos that promised the best sound ever. He watched as a young looking girl with long black hair walked onto the stage carrying a violin. She couldn't be any more than eighteen thought George, but from the applause coming from the audience this seemed to be the person they had all come to see.

She lifted a hand and the audience went quiet, 'I am so grateful to be here tonight. I am grateful to my parents . . .' She looked up towards the ceiling at this point and then slowly towards a couple sitting a few seats along from George. He noticed a spotlight and a cameraman focus on the couple, 'And I am so grateful to Mr. and Mrs. Philips.' George felt his wife grip his hand as the spotlight surrounded them and the cameraman moved in close. He held back a strong urge to wave at the camera and smiled at his wife, the expression on his face was asking her if he know who the girl was. His wife's expression said no. The girl smiled at them and then began playing her violin.

The calmness that her music instilled in George almost placed him in a trance, he had never heard anything like it, or even dreamed that music could be so soothing. When she had finished playing it seemed everyone had been lulled into the same state of relaxation, because the applause built up slowly then reached a deafening crescendo as the girl walked of the stage.

'Mr. and Mrs. Phillips my name is Lisa and these are my parents Mr. and Mrs. Cole.' George and his wife shook hands and exchanged pleasantries as they sat down for dinner. They had been shocked when the chauffeur drove straight to the Hilton hotel where he explained that they had been invited to dinner.

'I bet you're wondering what all this is about?' asked Lisa.

'We are a little curious,' replied George.

At that point Lisa reached under the table and handed George a small bag. 'I believe these belong to you?' George took the bag and looked inside, he pulled out the glasses and an old wallet that he had lost about six years ago.

'Where did you find these?' asked George, sounding surprised.

'My mother found them after she walked me to school just before Christmas. She would always stop on the way back through the park to leave food in the bushes for the ducks.' George looked at Lisa's parents who were smiling back at him. He began to feel angry as he recalled the morning he had been scared in the park and had run into a bush, losing his months wages as well as his Christmas bonus. He thought about the horrible Christmas he had had because his wife didn't believe him. She thought he had lost all the money playing cards at work, and that he had made up that silly ghost story.

'I had a horrible Christmas that year, why didn't you hand it in?' George aimed the question at Lisa's mother but Lisa answered for her.

'My mother was on her way to hand them in when she thought she would be better off checking the wallet for your address, in the hope that she could drop it straight back to your home . . . ' Lisa started to look slightly embarrassed. 'That was when she saw all the money in there.'

'Fifteen hundred pounds,' George added.

'That's right.' said Lisa, as she reached under the table again. She handed George an envelope. 'My mother knew she was wrong not to hand it in and she promised herself to pay you back one day.'

George looked at Lisa's mother as he opened the envelope. Inside were two first class tickets to Barbados, with a check for five thousand pounds. George handed the tickets to his wife, with a 'do you believe me now?' look on his face. His wife looked more embarrassed than Lisa did.

'This is very kind of you.' responded George, 'but if you can afford all this, what did you need my money for?' He aimed the question at Lisa's mother again.

Lisa tried to answer the question. 'At the time . . . '

George interrupted her. 'Please let her answer, I would like to hear how someone so rich could be so selfish that close to Christmas!' The memories of that Christmas were coming back stronger now and he could see the look on his grandchildren's faces as they opened the pitiful little presents that George was able to give them that year. George's wife squeezed his arm in an obvious attempt to get him to calm down. But all the shame and mistrust George suffered that Christmas spurred him on.

'I'm not a horrible person, Mrs. Cole . . . ' George looked straight into her eyes. 'But on that Christmas morning, as I watched my grandchildren open their cheap presents from my wife and me, I wished with all my heart, that who had ever found the money and didn't hand it in... '

He didn't want to say it but again the anger pushed him on. 'Well, I wished them a sudden death.' George watched the already fading smiles around the table disappear totally. Half of him felt bad but the other half didn't care. He grabbed the envelope from his wife, and chucked it towards Mrs. Cole as he got up to leave the table.

'I needed it six years ago!' he shouted. By now the whole restaurant had gone quiet and George felt all eyes were on him.

'Mr. Phillips . . . ' The tearful sound of her voice made George look at Lisa. 'I can understand your anger, but Mrs. Cole isn't my real mother.'

George sat down slowly and confused. Lisa continued. 'My mother found your address in your wallet, and was making her way to your house . . . ' Mrs. Cole held Lisa's hand. Lisa went on, 'to return your money, when she passed a music shop. The owner was placing a brand new violin in the window, the same one I played tonight.' George thought of the beautiful music she had played and even now it relaxed him. Lisa continued, 'My real mother wasn't rich at all, my father had died in a car crash a few years before and he had no life insurance or any real savings. My mother was finding it a real struggle to keep a roof over our heads.' Lisa tried to choke back her tears. 'When she saw that violin being placed in the window, the only thing I had ever wanted, she saw it as some kind of message from God, especially as the price tag was showing exactly 1,500 pounds.' Lisa managed a smile at the coincidence, 'Well, as you now know she bought me the violin and it was one of the best Christmases I've ever had.' She looked towards Mr. and Mrs. Cole. 'Not long after that, my mother collected me early from school with tears in her eyes, when I asked her what was wrong she eventually told me that she was going to be with daddy.'

Lisa read George's look. 'Mr. and Mrs. Cole are my foster parents, I went to live with them after my mum died two months later. Apparently she contracted cancer.' George looked away from Lisa, aware of the irony in her voice. Lisa went on, looking straight at George, 'Before she died, Mr. Phillips, she told me about the violin and how she was able to afford it. She made me promise to be the best violinist I could ever be, so that one day, I could honour her promise to God and return your money.'

Lisa eased the envelope back towards George. 'Please let me keep my promise to my mother Mr. Phillips. And let me say once again that I understand your anger and I forgive you for making such a wish.'

George wished that the floor would swallow him up, but then made a mental note to be more careful with what he wished for in future.

When Wishes Come True © Michael Grant 2000

The writings of American prisoners on Death Row have been celebrated in published collections such as *Out of the Night* and *Welcome to Hell*. One of the most infamous prisons to hold men sentenced to death is San Quentin, where **Freddie Taylor**, who wrote the following two short stories, has been held for over 14 years.

An African-American, he was born in Oklahoma. At the age of eight he was taken into State care, from where he graduated to prison and eventually Death Row. He began writing in 1992 . . .

'I was very sad upon receiving my second execution date. All I could think about was the wrong in my life, how what is seen to be wrong never leaves any opening for right . . . the society of America. One night it came to me—that all the good people of our world have their heroes, but who is there for the poor, the insane, the prisoner—and the wrong. So, to answer many questions I decided to allow Wrong to become a character—one who will come out and address the issues at hand. Many dudes who live within these walls have read Wrong and they all asked why I haven't published him. I didn't want to . . . until now'

George

Freddie Taylor

George's eyes were filled with tears. He turned his back to the Black guard who stood in front of his cell watching him. George only had three hours left in which to wait out his death sentence. For the last twenty years he had lived on Death Row and during that time he had gone through the whole appeal process. His last appeal had been denied and now the time of his death was drawing near. He had been offered his last meal. He refused it.

He had been offered a chaplain to comfort him during his last hours. He refused that too.

He had been offered the use of the telephone and he had just finished hanging up. The call had been more disturbing than he had ever expected. His mother had told him she couldn't let him go to his death without telling him a secret she had kept all her life. The secret was that George was adopted . . . and that one of his parents had been black.

George was on Death Row for the murder of a Black man. It had been what they call a 'Hate Crime.' He hadn't even known the man he had killed. From childhood on he had been taught to hate races other than White. He believed that the White race was superior. Now, looking at his hands with his back still turned to the guard, he asked himself if the news he had just received from his mother could really be true. How could it be? No! He couldn't believe it. Everything he had just heard must have been a lie.

George had blue eyes. He was six feet tall with a slim frame. He had blond hair. He looked at himself in the only mirror in the cage and began to wash his face very hard. Then he looked at himself in the mirror again. He heard the Black guard behind him begin to laugh.

George turned around, noticing for the first time that he didn't recognise this guard. Becoming angry he asked, 'What are you laughing at?'

He noticed the guard was wearing black shades and that he couldn't see the man's eyes.

'At you,' the guard said.

George walked up to his gate. 'So what's so funny spook?' he asked.

The guard bent over laughing harder.

This infuriated George. 'Spook!' he said louder. 'Spook! Spook!'

'Come on, George,' said the guard, becoming sober all at once. 'I know about it. '

George became confused. No voices could be heard other than his and the guard's. 'You know what?'

The guard took off his shades. 'Let me just say that I know your secret.' George was thrown off looking into the dark black eyes of the guard. He could hear his own heart beat as he stared into those eyes. He glanced at the name tag on the guard's uniform. 'Wrong' it read. He had never met the man before. George tried to reflect back in his mind if he had ever even heard one of his comrades mention the name of that particular guard.

'No,' Wrong said, seeming to read his mind and answering the question without it being asked. 'George, old boy, you know nothing of me and you can't intimidate me either.'

George said, 'Man, I have no time for games.' He suddenly realised how true those words were. He didn't have very much time left.

'Yes, you do, George,' said Wrong. 'You have enough time. Like I said . . . I know.'

George said, 'What do you mean?'

Wrong replied, 'Boy, right now, you need me to understand yourself.'

George felt like a little boy again. No Black man had ever talked to him in the way that Wrong was doing. He turned around and walked to his bunk and lay down. He wasn't going to listen to any Black guard. He never had and he wasn't going to start at this point in his life.

Wrong moved closer to the bars. He whispered, 'George John Smith, tell me how you feel, less than three hours from now you will be strapped to a table where you will be put to sleep like a dog. Yes, George, it's time for American justice to pay your bad ass back. Are you ready? Huh, George? Are you ready to be down with this death thing?'

George couldn't believe his ears. Here he was only hours away from death and this strange guard was messing with his head. He knew all about something nobody was supposed to know about and now he was talking about the execution. He raised up on his elbow and said, 'Man, if you are trying to mess with my head, you are doing a very good job of it.'

Wrong, without using any keys, opened up the cell door and walked right in. The door clanged shut behind him. He sat down next to George on the bunk.

George quickly felt drained. Becoming serious, Wrong said, 'I'm sorry, George. Sorry that your struggle had to come to this point. Sorry that you were caught between two different worlds. Sorry that your misguided teachings of rage and hate led you to take another human being's life. I'm also sorry for everything any man of color ever did to you that caused you to hate so much.'

Wrong looked at his own hands. Shaking his head he looked at George who lay curled up in his white jumpsuit. He asked, 'Did you really think that you were perfect?'

The question was so sudden and so unexpected that floods of tears sprang to George's eyes. As his head fell down, Wrong began to rub the back of his neck.

'Take it easy, George. Yes, your bridges are coming falling down. I'm sorry for that too. But please answer me. Did you think you were perfect?'

Sniffing, George replied, 'If thinking that I was better than Blacks, Jews, Mexicans, etc. meant I was perfect then yes, Mr. Wrong, I did.'

'Then tonight is your night, George,' Wrong said. 'Do you think it will end perfect?'

George looked in confusion at Wrong. 'I don't understand,' he said.

Wrong replied, 'Do you believe that this perfect system is going to adhere to you in your struggle against other races?'

'No.'

'So you see what's happening,' Wrong told him, 'You have become equal to Blacks and Jews. You are no different, George. I'm here to tell you you've been wrong.'

George stiffened. He said, 'I bet that by you seeing me cry you think that I'm some kind of punk.'

'No,' Wrong said. 'You are who you are. I believe that you cry not because you are less than a man or because you fear death. You are crying like every man does who comes through these prison doors and on into this waiting cell. Just like you, they were stripped of their identity at the end of their lives. You've been taught to hate all of your life. Now here at the end of your life you find you have been hating yourself. One last phone call has basically been your rebirth.'

Wrong stood up, opened the cell door and walked back out.

'Keep your head up, George,' he said. 'I'm sorry that you had to find out this way that you too are Black.'

Three hours later George was strapped to the table. He didn't cry. He looked around for Wrong but couldn't find him or even any eyes like his. Those that looked back at him were all as blue as his own, but there was no sympathy in those eyes because of that. The warden asked him, 'Mr. Smith, do you have any last words before your sentence is carried out?'

George said yes. Then he said:

Everywhere I look there are chains on my people.
Everything I've seen was the death of my people.
Everywhere I have been, I mistreated my people.
So this Justice today is _for_ my people.

Then he said in a low voice. 'I am Black and so are my people.'

He nodded at the warden saying 'Let's do this.' The last thing George heard before going into forever, dreaming, sleep was Wrong's voice: 'You did well, my son. Wrong will never encounter you again.'

The Man Nobody Knew

As he was walking toward the bank entrance, the people outside watched him. To the many eyes burning into his back, he didn't look like the type of character who was supposed to be going in. He seemed to stop as he entered. He glanced around, appearing to look up at the cameras over the security guards. It seemed as if he were counting the number of people in the bank.

Looking from right to left and left to right, he started walking toward the smallest line. Every single person in the bank could feel his presence. The last two men standing in the line in front of him fell quiet, their conversation about a fishing trip stopped.

The guard, with his trained eye and experience, began to move toward the door. He took up a 'ready position,' looking at the man in line and sizing him up. 'Yea,' he thought, 'Black man between the ages of 26 and 30, about five foot seven or five foot eight, weighing about 160 pounds. Blue jeans, wearing a pair of those damn tennis shoes. Black, short membership jacket.' He didn't like the jacket the most. 'Why would a Black man be in a bank wearing such a jacket?' he asked himself. 'Could it be that he has a gun under that jacket?' He looked at what he would see of the young Black man's face. He continued sizing him up. Hmmm, shaved. Hair cut short. 'Damn,' thought the guard. 'I can't see his eyes through those black shades.'

Before the thought had passed by the security guard's mind, the Black man reached up and took off his shades. He turned around and looked at the guard giving him 'the view'.

'Now,' thought the guard, 'all he has to do is make a wrong move. If he does I will be justified in blowing this fool away.' The line now had only four people left. The mind of the man standing right in front of the Black man in line was going wild. He felt that at any second all hell would break loose in the bank. He began to make the mental preparations for running. He started to sweat as he imagined the eyes of the young Black man burning through his back. The nervous man tried to gather his thoughts. He found he was thinking about his family.

Three people left.

The guard was ready. The tellers were all ready. And the Man Nobody Knew was ready.

Two people now left in line.

The man who was at the counter ahead of the Black man forgot why he was in the bank. His eyes kept darting from the bank teller to the door. 'I'm sorry, Miss,' he said, 'I've forgotten my check book.' Quickly he turned and walked away. The Black man walked up to the teller. At first she felt the same fear that everyone else in the bank was feeling and then suddenly it went away.

'Excuse me, Miss,' the Black man said, his voice friendly and innocent sounding. 'I've come to put some money into another person's account. I have the account number right here.' He reached towards his jacket zipper.

The guard had his hand on his gun.

He pulled the zipper down and reached inside his coat pocket. The teller saw the guard beginning to move out of the corner of her eye. She turned to tell him that everything was okay but the guard seemed not to notice her. All his attention was on thought-to-be-hostile man. The Black man was pulling out a long slip of paper when . . Bam! . . Bam! . . Bam! As if in slow motion the teller turned toward the Black man and saw that he was no longer standing there. There was blood all over the counter.

People were screaming and failing to the ground. The guard squatted with perfect aim, waiting for the suspect to get up. He could have sworn that this Black man was wearing a bullet-proof vest. So he shot him again. Bam!

Suddenly the young white female teller was running toward him screaming, 'Are you crazy? Are you crazy?' The guard was stunned. He didn't know what she was screaming about. Hadn't he just saved her life? But as she came closer he could hear her saying 'He wasn't armed. The man wasn't trying to rob the bank. You shot him for nothing.'

She turned and ran toward the bloody man lying on the floor. His eyes were open. He was lying on his side. His blood was pumping out onto the floor. She knelt down beside him and gently rolled him over onto his back. Sitting on the floor she placed his head in her lap. She could barely see him, her eyes were full of tears.

'God, what have we done?' she said. She looked down and rubbed his face tenderly.

He spoke to her and at first she could barely hear him. He repeated what he had said, 'Is this how you people treat all your customers?' He waited for her 'no.'

'What is your name?' he asked.

She couldn't remember for a moment and then told him 'Julie. My name is Julie.'

'Julie,' he said, 'I had a feeling something was wrong as I walked into your bank. I could have placed a bet that something was going to go down here. It just didn't cross my mind that it would be me.'

'What is your name?' Julie asked.

He smiled and coughed a little. 'My name is Wrong.'

'What?' she asked.

'My name is Wrong.'

She reached in his coat pocket and pulled out the paper. 'Who are these people?' she asked. 'Are they your family?'

He looked up at her with tears now in his eyes and said, 'No.'

'Well,' asked Julie, 'Will they be able to reach your family?'

Again he replied no. 'Julie,' he said, 'they don't know me either. Please, Julie, let me explain something to you. First of all I will die within the next ten minutes. Don't look surprised. It was fair game. I had a mission here on earth to help all of those who needed help. I'm responsible for the wrong of the needy. The 'wrong' of me, is the 'right' for others.'

'I have always been that person nobody knew. It's also a fact that once someone feels that they know me, my existence has to be destroyed.' His head turned towards the guard. Wrong whispered something which Julie had to bend over to hear. He said, 'Julie, that man killed me because he feared me. What he saw with his own eyes through mine was himself. He knew that I knew what he thought and Julie, still looking at Wrong, saw the life leave his eyes. Wrong died.

She looked up and around the bank. Real police were now there with their weapons drawn. She screamed at them, 'NO! It's wrong! It's wrong! It's all wrong!' She couldn't control her emotions, knowing as she did that this black man had died for all the wrong reasons.

As Wrong was being lifted from her lap a police woman walked up to her and asked 'Did he say what his name was?' Julie nodded saying very softly as she cried, 'The man nobody knew . . . Wrong.'

George and *The Man That Nobody Knew* © Freddy Taylor 2000

John Roberts explains that the first of these poems, written in HMP Risley, was inspired by a radio programme in which an old member of the Raj said the stars were so bright he could read by them. A keen poet, aged 34 and from Wales, he is in *HMP Risley*

Poems by John Roberts

The Times by Starlight – Sept 1939

Under the flooding starlight of central India
Come the uncanny sounds of night
Fanged? Forked? Ghost? Here, all is one.
A cry that may be death or life's beginning.

Cotton sticking, the sound suddenly stops.
And rushing in to fill the space
Swoops the pulsating weight of night.
With such immensity above,
Who would not believe in God?

Who would not conjure the dead, walk on coals,
Levitate the soul? Dare call a cow holy?
Well, why not. We are all just forms thrown
From the baked womb of this Indian earth.

Bewitching women, holy men –
All are struck by this stainless light.
And if in our parched air cruelty spores,
What is your excuse,
With your cold northern wars?

Ape

I have all that I want but my freedom
In the strained civility of this zoo.
Here is everything advantageous to life
Save the will to live.

Shall I describe a day? Doors open at 8
When the keepers serve the food.
Then we are allowed to move
Into the mock freedom of our cage.

It's large. They have wood for climbing on,
Tyres for swinging on, straw for lying on.
But all the time, one is uncomfortably aware
Of the constant observation.

The youngsters seem happy enough,
Gambolling away: they know no other life.
But memories swarm my face like flies –
Of the open, unfenced jungle skies.

Where one could climb to the tops of trees
And be along in the gentle sloughing
Of the bright blown leaves. Here,
If I lose my grip, I don't even die.

I just get laughed at. And my kin,
I so long to touch them. You know,
I would rather the hard fists of bad men
Than this soft civility slowly suffocating me.

At 12 we are ushered in for dinner; at two,
Let out again. Personally, I have ceased to be,
Don't set my life at a pin's fee –
Perhaps that's why I look so washed out.

I believe in plain speaking: let's not pretend
This does us any good, I am here
For your entertainment, because you have power
And like locking living creatures up.

Here we have no voice, which is convenient,
For I fear that this slow gnawing of the soul's base
Might in some manner constitute
A cruel and unnatural punishment.

Of course, I can speak only for myself,
As one born to climb, to roam, to attach:
In these deep brown brooding eyes you see
The remnants of a spirit born to be free.

It's 8 in the morning now. I won't ever be seduced
By the warmth of this soft hay bed.
I form my mind into a cup and scoop up
Sips to sustain me from the pool of my memory.

And for tomorrow? More of today.
I just thank my green God for sleep.

The Tramp

With the fortitude of a peasantry,
A feeling that the price isn't worth paying,
The stoic resignedness of a horse in the rain.
Not attributes I would necessarily recommend,
Still, we must play the hand we've been given.

A jaundiced eye, looking on the rich coldly,
The powerful laughingly, the pretty sadly:

It won't last, he says, yet here I stand
Doing what I do where I can.

The plant is in the grain,
It can never change,
The utopias and dystopias
Were ever a lie.

But please don't imagine
That I'm miserly and grim –
I envy no man nothing;
If I haven't got it
It's because I didn't really want it,
Its because this is who I am.

The man the little children mock,
The tainted wether of the flock.

Midsummer '99

Summer's still wind settles on the land,
Slow pooling, swirling, a self-setting fire.
Structures may be wrought, prisons built,
Morals taught. But here in the long field

Where little eddies rise, spiriting grass,
Twitching the nose of a hare in its form.
One feels that along with the pollen is borne
The seed life, forever set to spawn –

Even as time turns to reveal the human wreck,
A hull left for fishes to infest.

Prosevad

They're coming to draw the joy from the world.

An anonymous man in white, large syringe in hand,
Flanked by men in uniforms,
Led by men in suits.

Mobiles had rung with a chorus of tinny tunes –
They'd got a live one, Sector 8,
Innocently amusing himself.

The uniforms held him, the suits read to him.
The syringe was struck,
And his poor joy was withdrawn.

Across his forehead, in lurid read,
They stamped, perfunctorily,
The word 'sane'.

And then their chirrupy pockets chirrped again.

Buddha

I am beginning to think that it is enough
To lapse along pleasantly with the days

Occasionally I am troubled by the odd thought rising
From the sluggish pool of my mind,
But the blaggard is soon put down.

There are rainy days when the news of the world
Ripples my peaceful repose;
But the news soon dissolves in the depth of my being.

Is this any way to live? I must confess
There is little choice, between the sides of these banks
In this forgotten ox-bow of life.

I let shadows of clouds pass over me,
See martins busy in their life-fight
Whilst I drift gently, this way and that.

Never getting very far, swirling slowly back.
For months on end I gaze at a tree
Which casts its fascinating shadow over me.

But occasionally (perhaps twice a year
When I am awoken by the cold stars' staring eyes)
I think I hear the distant slough of the sea.

It is only then, in the amphibious drift
Between wakefulness and sleep,
That I find myself thinking pointedly –

Of the salt shock of lived life,
Of the shifting, glittering colour of life
With gulls crying sharp shrieks into ears.

And then I wish I wasn't here.
I really wish I wasn't here.

All poems in this section © John Roberts 2000

Looking Back

Looking Back

The nostalgic side of life on the run in Ireland is recalled here by **Tony Savage,** from Long Bay Jail, south of Sydney, Australia. He describes himself as 'a computer expert, a greenie, a failed political candidate and a champion lawn bowler who loves good wine, food and friends.' None of which are available in his present surroundings.

Irish Eyes

Tony Savage

Irish skies were crying as I crossed the Ha'penny Bridge for what I thought was the last time. I was dejected, depressed, home sick and just about broke. I was also on the run from Canberra's Keystone Cops.

The Ha'penny Bridge crosses the Liffey in the heart of Dublin. A steel, arched footbridge from the Temple Bar to the main shopping district of Dublin where I was off to buy a shillelagh as a souvenir of a wonderful time in Ireland. I never did get that shillelagh. I was side tracked at the Keg. A pub. A working man's pub. A real Irish pub in real Ireland with none of your airs and graces of the plastic Irish pubs which are competing with McDonalds in the race to infest every corner of the globe. My excuse for entering this esteemed establishment was the rain, a fairly constant companion in this land of the shamrock.

I ordered my first Guinness just before the real Irish working men left their real Irish work site, across the road, and just before the real Irish working men took over the real Irish working men's pub. By the time the place filled up my first Guinness for the day had arrived.

The charm and beauty of Irish pubs is enhanced by the black stuff served in them. The stuff with the priest's collar. A good Guinness can take up to eight minutes to pour and settle and to carve the shamrock in the foam which delights the new visitor to Ireland. This normally gives ample time for the stranger to become acquainted with his fellow thirsty but patient members of the clientele. Not like Australia where the beer is cold and wet and poured as quickly as possible. I've seen times when I've walked into my local and by the time I've got to the bar, Deirdre—all barmaids are called Deirdre in Australia—had my schooner poured and my change sitting next to it for the ten dollar note she knew I would be paying with. This allows no time for the niceties of passing the time of day with someone you've never met in all of your life before.

The someone I'd never met in all of my life before, I met on that rainy day in Dublin at The Keg . . .

Forearms like Popeye and as pretty as Bluto. And a thirst like nothing I'd seen before or since. He taught me how to drink Guinness. I thought I could but I was wrong. As soon as the first landed 'same again' came the cry.

And he was right, or almost. It was a bit of a push for me to finish mine before the second Guinness came, but I played the game and 'same agained' as good as he did. Lunchtime finished for the working Irishmen in their Irish workingmen's pub and all but my Popeye/Bluto mate took off back to their Irish workingmen's work sites. Peter or was it Padraeg or was it Padre, I don't know—the Guinness was starting to take hold and I know what actually happens in this story and I can guarantee that I was unwell the next morning and had missed quite a lot of what actually did happen. Irish will do. Irish decided he'd stay to make sure the poor Aussie didn't get lonely or get led astray. We sat at the bar and talked and talked and skited and bragged about the beauty of our countries and the rugged beauty of our women. Or was it the rugged beauty, never mind, you get the idea. Lots of talk and two thirsty blokes 'same againing' at the correct moments in our conversation. I knew this was my last sojourn into the daytime drinking habits of the Irish bar life of Dublin, so I sat back, enjoyed and watched the last of my Irish punts turn into Irish pints and pence.

Around about Guinness number six the tallest man I had ever seen ducked through the front door of The Keg and sauntered, as only men over seven foot can saunter, up to the bar.

He ordered 'A simple glass of water please and not the frozen stuff through the bar pipes. I have a terrible tooth you see I'll have one out of the tap in your kitchen if you please—ahh you're a fine young man'.

And off scampered the fine young man to do the right thing for this very tall and obviously very thirsty Irish giant.

No sooner than the fine young man was gone than the Giant of Ireland whipped out the long-nosed pliers and proceeded in trying to separate the poor box from the connecting chain connected to the anchor set in the concrete floor behind the bar.

I'm sure I've told you I was on Guinness number six. Around about Guinness number four I grow eight inches and weigh an extra seventy-five pounds. I was more than ready for this bloke. Even though I was now six foot three and 300 pounds he still had seventeen inches and probably 150 pounds on me. Nevertheless I grabbed the arm with the hand holding the pliers and stunned him into not hitting me straight away by using my fine accent. I complained in my best Strine 'What the fuck are you doing?' He then started to lift his hand holding the pliers, which unfortunately was connected to the arm that I was holding.

It was then that I found out Irish's profession. He was a scaffolder. And as all Irish scaffolders know, an Irish scaffolder is not an Irish scaffolder unless he has his Irish scaffolders' scaffolder hammer with him. It's an ugly brute of a piece of metal used to knock the shit out of uncooperative scaffold pipes. And my mate Irish used all of his good looks, judgement and Popeye forearms to introduce the head of his scaffolders' hammer to the back of the Irish Giant's hand. It was only after the Irish Giant took off screaming and bleeding towards the front door and then knocked himself senseless on the top of the door frame that my mate said, 'I got the right hand then'. I 'same agained' and continued a wonderful afternoon inside The Keg.

As an aside to this story, my Irish mate got me a job as a scaffolders' mate on the building site. I was to follow him around with a bit of pipe and a spare scaffolder's hammer. It was only when I finally got out onto some scaffolding and it started to sway away from the building that I realised I was terrified of heights. Irish sacked me as a scaffolders' mate and re-hired me as a scaffolders' follower. I was to follow the foreman and whenever he came within cooee of the scaffolders' card table I'd yell out 'Liam have you seen the boys?' All this and £27 an hour. I spent the next two weeks half-way up the newest mall in Henry Street luxuriating in being able to afford Guinness and companionship and still putting pennies in my pocket to fund my life on the run.

The Irish Giant was a very real Irish man from up in the North. He was renowned, or more properly infamous, for his petty thievery and burglary throughout the whole island of Ireland. Sadly he died a little while back. One of the colourful characters of a colourful country—all of us the sadder for his passing.

I went back to The Keg Christmas 1997. It had been turned into one of the original plastic Irish pubs that the breweries are so keen to have all over Ireland so that when a tourist visits they can see that their 'genuine Irish pub' in Milan is the same as the plastic pub in Dublin.

Many prisoners who write delve back into their childhood, to times when life was often much happier and escapades were innocent—if hard to explain to parents. Here, **Stephen Lewtas** from the Wolds, tells the story of his efforts to obtain a pair of prized monkey boots.

Monkey Business

Stephen Lewtas

'Stephen, I won't tell you again. Get up for school, NOW!'

My dreams floated away like balloons on a gentle breeze as Mam's voice carried up the stairs and along the landing to my bedroom.

'Do you hear me?'

'Yeah, Yeah, I'm getting' up now!' I croaked.

I whipped the sheets back and leapt out of bed, snatching my patched up school trousers from the chair in the corner and sliding into them. My shirt was where I'd left it the day before, crumpled up and tossed on the floor in the middle of the room. I quickly put it on and tried to ignore the fact that it was two sizes too big and had three buttons missing. I mean, considering it had been worn by four of my older brothers for school before finally reaching me, it wasn't in too bad a condition.

That was the trouble with being second youngest in a family of six boys, by the time the hand-me-downs landed in my lap, they were usually torn to shreds and beyond repair. Poor Mick, who was the youngest, had it even worse. By the time I had passed them on to him they would probably be unfit for the rag man to take. But today, I didn't care. Today was special. Today was my birthday!

I reached under the bed and pulled out my battered and torn baseball pumps. They had certainly seen better days that was for sure. How I longed for a pair of monkey boots. All the other kids were wearing them. I must have been the only one in the playground who never had a pair but with Dad out of work, and Mam struggling to make ends meet, I didn't want to burden them with my cravings for a pair of monkey boots.

'Are you up yet?' Mam's voice floated up the stairs again and after a quick swill, I made my way down to the kitchen for breakfast. Mam was at the grill making toast whilst my brothers sat around the table shovelling cornflakes down their mouths. As I walked in, George, the eldest, glanced at my shirt.

'Isn't that the shirt I wore for school?' he asked around a mouthful of Kellogg's.

'Yeah, it is,' I replied.

'Fuckinell,' said Peter, the second eldest. 'I had that on when I had that fight with Tommo to see who was the cock of the school. Look, it's still got the blood stain on where I broke his nose.'

Sure enough, there it was. A now brown stain on the left sleeve.

'Shurrup and eat yer breakfasts,' barked Mam. 'And cut that swearing out.'

Peter went back to his cornflakes as I plonked myself down in a chair and filled a bowl for myself. I glanced at them all one by one. No-body was paying me any attention. How could they not remember? It was my birthday and nobody even knew! I was devastated.

'I don't want any breakfast Mam,' I said sulkily. ' I'm goin to school.'

With that I dropped my spoon in the bowl, pushed my chair back and sloped out of the kitchen. I just caught the sound of Peter's voice as I grabbed my blazer from the banister in the hall and slammed out of the front door.

'What's wrong with him?' he asked. 'At least it wasn't my blood on the shirt.'

My usual route to school took me through the outdoor market on the Estate and I loved it. Sometimes I would leave early so I could watch the stall holders setting up, and laying out their goods. Me and the other kids on the Estate would rob these stalls blind on the weekends to earn our sweet money. With unemployment rife and our parents struggling it was hard for them to afford to give us any pocket money, so we made our own by pilfering. The stall owners had got wise to us after a while and it was becoming harder and harder to have them over, but one way or another, we usually ended up with a bob or two for a few sweets.

That morning as I trudged past all the market stalls on my twelfth birthday, I remember feeling so sorry for myself that the biggest bag of sweets in the world could not have cheered me up. Then I saw them, right in front of me, sitting proudly on top of a shoe box on a stall we had robbed silly, the objects of my sweetest dreams. A brand new pair of black, leather, screaming to be snatched, monkey boots!

I had to have them, no matter what. I was getting those monkey boots if it killed me. If they were a size or two too big it wouldn't matter. I'd just wear three pairs of socks. And if they were too small I'd cut off my toes to make them fit. What ever, one thing was for sure. I would not get a better opportunity than this. I looked at the stall owner, he was unloading his van and spreading his merchandise about the stall. Each time he turned his back to grab another box he was blind to what was happening behind him.

As casually as my racing heart would allow, I strolled over to the stall next to his and pretended to be browsing at the cheap household goods that were displayed. The shoe-stall owner turned around with his next box and plonked it on the stall paying me no attention. Then as he turned his back for the next, I struck.

Darting forward, I plucked the monkey boots from the box they were sitting on and bolted off, but I had mistimed my swoop and was seen by the owner as he turned around with his next box.

'STOP HIM!' he bellowed, 'SOMEBODY STOP HIM!'

The market was empty except for a few early morning bargain hunters and a couple made a grab for me but I slipped by them and dodged my way through the small crowd. With my prize tucked under my arm, I sprinted out of the aisle and headed for my familiar escape route. Over a nearby wall and across a few gardens before disappearing into a block of flats and emerging out the other side onto our street. Panting, I trotted down the alleyway leading to the back of the house and quietly opened the gate before slipping into the shed and closing the door behind me.

I'd done it! At last, I finally had a pair of monkey boots. It seemed that this birthday was going to be a good one after all. I sat on the floor and tore my old baseball pumps from my feet, the smell of new leather filling my nostrils as I slid the new boot on to my left foot. I quickly laced it up before snatching the other one and slipping it on to my right. It was then that I noticed something was wrong. It didn't feel right. I stood up and looked down at my feet.

Oh no! Please no! But there was no mistaking what I could see. The boots were both left feet! I couldn't believe it. I was absolutely devastated.

So set was I on keeping the boots that I convinced myself that if I turned one foot inwards slightly, nobody would notice the difference and I decided to hold onto them. I crept out of the shed and down the garden path, stopping at the dustbin to stuff my tattered old baseball pumps inside. Then I shuffled my way to school to show off my new boots.

I was fooling nobody. All that day I was the butt of the other kids' jokes as they nudged each other and snickered at my two left monkey boots. I couldn't wait for the school bell to go. The last lesson was history but far from concentrating on the Battle of Hastings, I was more interested in getting home to rescue my baseball pumps from the bin before the bin men came. Finally, it rang and I raced from the classroom and tore up the road for home.

All I was thinking was, please, please, let them still be there. It took me about five minutes to sprint the mile or so to the house before finally, and sweating like a pig, I burst through the back gate and snatched the lid off the bin.

'Shit.'

I was too late. It was empty. What was I going to do? How could I explain to mam why I had no pumps? I was in deep trouble and there was no way out.

I resigned myself to the forthcoming slippering and slouched into the house with my head bowed. The kitchen was empty.

' Mam, it's me, Stephen. I'm home.' Silence.

' Mam, I've gotta tell you something.' I shuffled across the kitchen to the living room door and pulled it open.

'SURPRISE!'

I nearly jumped out of my skin as the room erupted with an explosion of noise. A sea of faces greeted me with pats on the back and a ruffle of my tatty blonde hair. Everybody was there. All my brothers, my one and only sister Lilly, my mates, my cousins.

Mam's face appeared in front of me.

'Thought we forgot didn't yer, lad?' She laughed before planting a sloppy kiss on my cheek. Her hands, which had been hidden behind her back, emerged with a package which she thrust into my hands.

'Happy Birthday son.' she said.

I smiled, full of the joy of being loved and appreciated by all my friends and family as I tore the wrapping from the parcel. My mouth fell open as I looked down at my present. 1 couldn't believe what I was looking at. But it was true.

Yes, she had bought me a brand new pair of gleaming black monkey boots.

'But Mam,' I spluttered, 'how did you afford them?'

'Oh it's all right son, I got them cheap on the market,' she said.'You do like them, don't you?' They're better than them old things you've been wearing.'

As she spoke, her eyes slid down to my feet expecting to see my old baseball pumps, only to be greeted by the sight of my two left-footed monkey boots looking back at her. I had forgotten all about them in the excitement!

' Erm, I can explain Mam,' I stammered. ' Honest.'

' This better be good Stephen,' she frowned.

' This better be good.'

The welcome home party has been a feature of many a film or TV episode, with friends and acquaintances gathering to pay their respects to the prisoner who has been released after years inside. Here, *Bogart's Coming Out Party* by **Ian Watson** of The Wolds takes a slightly different view—a light-hearted account of a prisoners' reunion.

Bogart's Coming Out Party

Ian Watson

Micky opened the roadmap and loose pages tumbled into the footwell of the car, joining unpaid parking tickets, old crisp packets, sandwich wrappers and the odd crushed can or two. 'Christ Dad! You could have cleaned the inside up a bit. Have you no shame?'

'Who's going to see it?' I argued. 'The party's in the pub not the car.'

'But what if we have to give someone a lift?'

'No lifts—we're sleeping in this thing tonight with the keys tucked safely behind the bar.'

'Can't we stay at Bogart's—after all he invited us?' Mick asked.

'Mick, there's 36 already planning to doss at Bogart's plus another six chancing it in the shed with his pony.'

'Bogart and the lads won't mind me coming, will they?' This was Micky's next worry.

'Relax son—course they won't mind. They all want to meet you. They've heard all about you and they've seen you on visits. You're famous for humping that bird on top of the wheelie bin in Manchester and finishing two streets away from where you started.' Mick squirmed with embarrassment.

'It was only 50 yards away, not two streets . . .and we were on a hill.'

'Do you ever hear from her?' I probed.

'No. With the snide address and phone number I gave her she'd need to be called Clouseau to track me down.' Mick giggled at the memory.

'From Bogart's directions The Diamond should be at the bottom of the hill.' Sure enough seconds later we were parking on the dust bowl outside the pub.

'Bloody hell!' spluttered Micky. 'Does Norman Bates keep his mother upstairs? Surely, this can't be a place of enjoyment?'

'Yes son. Welcome to the legendary Diamond. There's Bogart's taxi at the side.'

I pointed towards the four tone blue Sierra with optional dust and alloy ashtrays—value for insurance purposes, about 50 quid.

We locked the car and a sharp sea breeze whipped the car park dust into our eyes. We'd only been there three seconds and already our shiny shoes were dirty. Micky wiped his on the back of his Levis and together we stepped over the threshold. We turned left out of the evening sunlight and back several decades. The narrow room stretched some 50 feet with a dark mahogany bar running its full length. The old bar mirrors advertised Nimmo's Ales which I knew hadn't been brewed for 20 years. The shelves had promotional glasses and display bottles of Babycham and Cherry B. Mick thought he was in a museum. Sitting on the bar was a redundant pie-warmer with a lifeboat charity box stored behind its glass doors. Also, stacked on the bar, were some plastic drums of detergent and boxes of toilet tissue—the waxy kind I'd not seen since infant school. The walls were covered with framed photographs of past pub outings, a calendar from the local tyre centre, and in the corner was a wall-mounted telephone with dozens of numbers scribbled on the surrounding, yellowing wallpaper.

'No party here,' we concluded.

We turned right into the next large room decorated in various shades of nicotine. The exceptions were the plush red Dralon stools which, with all their cigarette burns, looked like Emmenthal cheeses. At a rectangular table sat a domino school of ex-pitmen, each in shiny suit trousers, collarless shirts and neckerchiefs.

They sat along side a dart-board with its stuffing bursting out, and above them were notices of inter-pub games. The tables of the local darts, domino and pool leagues—the Geordie Triathlon—showed that The Diamond wasn't too clever at any of their pastimes.

'Looking for Bogart's do?' asked one of the players from under his checked tweed cap. With a definite note of affection at the mention of Bogart, he continued 'It's in the main lounge, just follow the noise. By the way while you're here—would you like to buy some fresh lettuce lads?'

He produced a crumpled Netto bag containing a fresh lettuce and black soil in about equal measures. 'It's cheap enough—just dug up.'

His neighbour chipped in. 'So fresh, the guy whose allotment it's from doesn't know it's gone yet.' 'I'm OK for veg thanks,' I replied.

'Owt else you need?' asked another. 'Tabs, diesel—a pound a gallon?'

'Let me dream on it, I'm here for the drinking,' I laughed.

Finally, we'd made it to the main lounge. It was the size of a Methodist chapel. It would have taken most of the output from the old pit just to heat it. But it was hot with the warmth of over a hundred bodies. Some were stood in small knots drinking and a few of the younger lasses were bopping to a bit of Tamla on the disco that Bogie had laid on. I cast my gaze around the gathering but I heard him before I saw him—amazing since he's six foot seven. He strode towards me, arms spread wide.

'Now then Marra—isn't this the business? Great you could make it. Eeh I'll be buggered, it's the first time I've seen you without a blue and white striped shirt.'

'Aye and I'll be a long time till I buy any more blue clothing,' I rapped back.

His white hair and beard were both well trimmed, framing his ruddy complexion. Matching strands of curly hair poured out the top of his silk shirt while his head leaned slightly to the left, almost as if it was too heavy for his neck. He was just as I remembered him, all those evenings walking around the prison field.

He turned towards our kid and started pumping his arm unwittingly crushing young Micky's hand.

'Eh—you must be Micky—I've heard some stories about you. See that young lass over there in the Labatt's T-shirt?' Micky nodded wondering what was coming next. 'That's our lass, me daughter. Now her and wheelie bins are off limits—do you understand?'

Our kid went the same shade of white as the blown vinyl on the walls. Bogart shook with laughter and left us to patrol his various guests. In one group were his taxi drivers; in another, the staff from his cafe and chip shop; then there were the lads who operated his hot dog trolleys, enjoying a night off. Finally, there were those of us who'd spent the last couple of years with the big fella. Bogart had been Number One in the prison kitchens because of his catering experience and his hygiene certificate from the hot-dog operation. He might as well have drawn the principal officer's salary so great was his influence and charisma in the jail.

Before Bogart's reign, the prison kitchen had won an award for a 'Healthy Options' campaign. To prove this, there was a framed photo of the Governor receiving a certificate from someone dressed as a carrot. All this had been faithfully recorded by local television. Bogart, being of the cardiac school of cuisine had changed all this and soon chips were even an option at breakfast. He catered for all tastes, even putting strawberry jam in the porridge and rice pudding so that the gays would like the pink colour.

He recruited me from induction, to work in the bakery and serve the bread and butter—'The Breadman of Alcatraz' he called me. What a crew we were! The butcher, nicknamed the Terminator, was finishing off a life sentence surrounded by enough knives to arm Galatasaray. A poisoner did the vegan meals and an arsonist was in charge of the boiler house.

I looked around the room—all Top Shop, Matalan and Grattan's catalogue. If you'd taken these three out of the clothing equation it would have been a nudist meeting. In the midst of everyone, the big fella was opening a neatly wrapped parcel topped with a dainty bow and accompanied by a greeting card with a teddy bear on the front.

Inside the parcel was a Fisher Price teething ring. 'Bastards,' he proclaimed, putting the toy on a table with about 30 others. Then the penny dropped: Bogie had got his time for stealing a container of these toys. This was everyone sharing a quiet joke at the big fella's expense—but he didn't mind in the least.

Then we clapped eyes on Thumbria, at 22 the youngest of our HMP colleagues. He looked a million dollars in his expensive gear. I'd always thought he'd put a bit away. He was talking to a bird in her thirties who was hanging on to his every word. You could tell she thought Christmas had come early. Thumbria had been working in one of these furniture hypermarkets and for 18 months he'd relocated both cash and stock as the whim took him. The police had put his gain at £70 K and Thumbria was more than happy with their mathematics.

Paddy had called him Thumbria and it had stuck. Paddy was doing a three for a building tax scam and was useless with names but great with places. He called most people by some abbreviation of the town from which they came. Dave being from Northumbria copped for Thumbria. I was Cheshire. There was a lad in the jail from Peterlee, and this had totally confused Paddy.

I gave Thumbria a warm handshake and introduced him to our Micky. 'Who's the bird?' I asked, whispering in his ear to make myself heard above the music.

'Just a local lass—one night only. I've started a new job, with new girlfriend, new address etc.—you know the dance. The new bird back home doesn't know I've been on my holidays last year so I thought this party with you all here might be a bridge too far.'

Bogart's daughter came over and I left her latching on to Mick and Thumbria. They were drinking lager straight from the bottle. I shuddered at the thought of all the rats that had probably pissed on those bottles while they were stored in the yard of The Diamond. At least drinkers would be immunised against the plague by the end of the evening.

I looked around and let the hubbub of the room wash over me. Here we all were, all four of us, only the Terminator was missing, here in spirit but back at base and finishing his life sentence. Even he had promised to ring before 'bang up' to send his best. We'd thought we were fixture's in that jail, though in reality it hadn't been that long for any of us. I can hear the roll call in the kitchen, the screw even calling us by our nicknames—Alcatraz, Terminator, Bogart, Thumbria and One Blonk. But we were here and this was the night we had often talked about—the night when we'd finally get together, convince each other it was all over and have a laugh and a drink about it.

In many ways freedom had been an anticlimax and I realised now that these guys were my truest mates—people who'd shared adversity with me—who'd shared their last strands of dry baccy or a few units on a phonecard when you needed a phone call.

I was bumped back into reality by One Blonk digging me in the ribs and giving me the biggest hug of the evening. I'd always had a soft spot for old OB. He was older than the rest of us and in truth we'd all looked after him a bit. He got his nickname after his pit accident in which he'd lost an eye. He'd been unable to get comfortable with a glass eye so had just left a blank socket. For this reason, plus the fact he was captain of the domino team, he'd been given the nickname One Blonk from the day of the accident. He was wealthy but what Yorkshire folk called careful. In fact was so careful about making VAT payments that he had just got an 18 month stretch as proof.

With his original compensation, he'd bought an aircraft carrier, with the aim of scrapping it for the metal. Until they started breaking it up, it was OB's boast that, for three weeks he had the eighth largest navy in the world by tonnage. His purchase had proved a wise one when he'd found the hull stockpiled with unused metal beds, the sale of which repaid his original outlay. The carrier was pure profit.

Not one to relax on a fortune he'd then built an hotel—entirely from stolen materials it seemed. He'd nicked six floors of scaffolding from a hotel on Scarborough sea-front, dismantling it 24 hours before the rightful owners arrived to do the same. He'd even demolished a small chapel overnight for the hotel's foundations and the pulpit had been made into a bar in his own home.

'What you up to One Blonk?' I hardly dared to ask.

'Glad you asked,' he warmed to the conversation immediately. 'Have you ever realised that it's impossible to be buried with your pets in this country? Well I've brought 50 acres from the Coal Board and put in for planning permission for a private cemetery for pets and humans. Got the idea from my aunt in Salt Lake City.'

'What your chances of getting it past the planners?' I asked.

'Virtual certainty,' he grinned conspiratorially. 'If they don't pass it they know I'll open the biggest temporary gypsy site in Europe. They won't want that on their doorsteps, will they? If they turn it down next week, the invitations will go out to travellers from Cork to Kosovo to bring their trailers to One Blonk's.' We both dissolved in gales of laughter.

'Do you still think much about jail?' I continued.

'Never a day goes past without it gripping me,' he confided and the mood changed. 'Especially the early days—they haunt me. The long bang-ups, the cockroaches, those bastards on the staff . . . then you lot came along . . . different memories—more like me National Service days tonight. This doesn't feel like cons getting together—it feels like it's us showing them that we're decent people with decent friends who can have a good time.'

'Do you think we'll get a lock-in tonight?' I tried to cheer up the conversation.

'Do you know ' he continued, 'I still feel a shudder when I hear a bolt sliding in on a door. I don't think it'll ever leave me.'

Thumbria came and joined us. He and One Blonk were close, like father and son in age. The young fella put a protective arm around One Blonk's shoulder.

'Is the vodka okay for you OB?' he teased.

'Aye and its cheaper than the 20 quid a bottle charged in the nick,' came the reply.

Thumbria had had a good racket going. He'd had a trusted job going out of the prison gates each day to service all the fire extinguishers, including those down the road in the screws' social club. He'd come back through the gates with everything from vodka to the *Racing Post* inside the empty extinguishers all collected from pre-arranged hidey-holes. He'd bring them all back to the little cabin the prison provided.

From there he'd ring his Mum on his mobile phone which lived and was recharged in the cabin, and he'd re-order stock. Thumbria told O. B about his new job, new girlfriend, new life and the old man promised if they ever bumped into each other in Newcastle he'd never mention where they'd met. 'In that case, I might invite you all to my wedding,' promised Thumbria. 'Though one or two of you might be difficult to explain.'

At ten o'clock, the lager ran out so Bogart dispatched his taxi for two trips to Asian Simon's 'Eight 'til Late'. When Simon heard whose party it was he loaded every available can, saying Bogart could settle later. He shut the shop early and became a welcome addition to the party.

Simon had six daughters and longed for a son. He promised a party no one would ever forget if Gita ever obliged him with a son. By eleven o' clock all the beer, even the mild, had run out. Partygoers were moving to more exotic and ingenious choices of drink. One table was experimenting with Gin and Castaway while even the Landlady's Christmas pudding rum bottle had appeared.

By midnight the lounge was knee deep in discarded cans, paper-plates, cocktail sticks which all crunched underfoot. Everyone sang along to Gloria Gaynor's 'I will survive'. No one was moving to the exits. Except that is, the four old domino players from the back snug. Bogart had sent them drinks through all evening and they were full of food from the buffet.

One of them had upset the Landlady by suggesting that Bogart take over the catering for the darts and dominoes teams in future.

'We could get kicked out the league on account of Annie's Spam sandwiches.' He teased the old landlady who feigned offence. In truth Annie had enjoyed having the pub full just like the old days when her late husband, Henry, ran things.

The old domino players staggered into the night air sniffing the ozone and looking at the night sky for weather prospects. Outside were two police minibuses, each with four occupants, all aware of who was at the party and why it was taking place.

'Show your faces,' the old desk sergeant had told the eight bobbies at the start of the night shift. 'Take some breathalysers. We might get lucky and check tax and tyres on all those motors.'

'Now then here's the Durham Light Infantry,' said a burly copper in the front passenger seat of the first minibus. 'Are there many in tonight?'

'No comment,' said a practised old Henry Lancashire.

'Ere lads you'd better get on the radio, you'll need more taxis than this. Twenty-two Stevenson Street, driver, stopping at the Rose of India for our lass's prawn biryani,' said Albert Curle getting into the vehicle. 'Fuck off, this in't a taxi,' said a weary copper as Albert settled into a back seat.

'What else is it—it's got a load of seats and a light on the top,' slurred Albert in what he thought was his most reasonable voice.

'Come on,' he continued oblivious to the driver's mounting temper, 'It's a decent fare and I'll chuck in three lettuces as a tip—can't be fairer than that.'

'Out, or you're nicked,' was the curt reply.

'What's the charge—selling lettuce in a built up area—is it?' That tipped the driver's emotional scales.

'Right smart arse—you're nicked,' and he clamped the handcuffs on old Albert.

'Fine by me,' beamed Albert. 'The cop shop's just over the road from the house—saves me old legs. 'Parrot' Hancock is desk sergeant tonight and he's the wife's cousin so I reckon it'll be a ticking off and home—like a side bet on it?'

Albert's three domino companions were less than pleased to see the old guy cuffed up and moved closer to protest. One of the officers had an Alsatian dog straining on the leash. 'Move back or I'll let the dog loose,' he warned.

Henry Lancashire looked at the dog and from his carrier bag he pulled out a catering-size bag of pork scratchings, which he'd taken from the back of Annie's bar while her back had been turned. He opened the bag and split the pork scratchings in front of the dog. The dog surged forward to demolish this unexpected snack almost dislocating the shoulder of his handler.

Back inside The Diamond, the barking of the police-dog had aroused partygoers. Sarah Rattigan had looked through the brown Dralon curtains and shouted to everyone. 'The dibbles outside arresting the domino team.'

Everyone poured out of the party to see what was happening. The sight of a hapless Albert in the back of the minibus seemed to light the touchpaper. With Bogart at the head of things, everyone swarmed round the two vehicles and started rocking them. In no time, two police drivers were hanging upside down in their seatbelts and Albert was sat on the ceiling of the van complaining of feeling dizzy.

Annie had spirited the police dog away and it was out the back of the pub drinking milk laced with rum to keep out the night chill. Shortly, it would have its best sleep since puppyhood. At the front of the pub, confusion reigned. Police reinforcements were rushing to the scene. There wasn't an air of malice or hostility—no one really knew what all the fuss was about so all the struggling had been a storm in a teacup.

Our kid had sloped off with Debra, Bogart's daughter. She'd persuaded him her dad was really a pussycat and alcohol had weakened his resistance to her chat up lines.

Annie was locking up the pub while making tea and toast for the police. She'd had her best night's takings in years—she'd have to completely restock at the cash and carry in the morning.

For us, it was like old times. All four of us back behind bars at the local nick. We looked around—Bogart, One Blonk, Thumbria and myself, Alcatraz with Henry Lancashire in the cell next door. Even the Terminator was there in spirit.

Next morning it was crap toast, flea bites from the blankets, microwaved sausages, cautions and splitting hangovers—all the ingredients of a proper party.

Bogart's Coming Out Party © Ian Watson 2000

It is sometimes assumed—wrongly—that *Prison Writing* is interested only in prisoners who write about prison. **John Wrigglesworth,** a lifer now in Channings Wood, gives the lie to that assumption in the following account of a childhood experience in Nigeria. John has had work published in three earlier issues of PW.

King of the Bees

John Wrigglesworth

From the moment I stepped off the plane at Abuja airport, and was struck by the intense heat from the mid-day sun, my heart was captured by Nigeria. All my senses were bombarded, in that instant, by the rich mixture of colour, sound and the aromas, a combination of sickly sweetness and comfortable decay. It left a taste in the very depths of my soul that still haunts my dreams today, more than 30 years on. For me Nigeria was a place of magic. Such a short period of my life, just a few incredible months, but a time that changed my world forever and a moment in my existence where my horizons were expanded beyond belief. Nigeria was to prove an amazing place.

It all happened so quickly, so fast in fact that as a family we didn't really have enough time to take it all in, before we had to do it. Not that it would have made much difference anyway because I, my younger brother and even younger sister were too young to take an active part in such a big decision anyway. Although, to be fair to my parents, they did make some effort to include us, but it was already a done deed by then. It was my father's calling, a need to do something with his life that really mattered, he said. He came home one day from work and told us about the new life we were all about to start. A few weeks later we were on the plane to Nigeria. It was a great adventure for anyone, but prior to that flight, the furthest my family had been from our Yorkshire roots was a day trip to Blackpool. My father had been given the opportunity to teach at a remote village in the north-eastern highlands of Nigeria. It was at an ex-Ministry house that had been bequeathed to our local church when a member of our congregation died. Full of zeal, the church elders had decided to take on the process and my father had jumped in dragging his wife and us three children with him. All we really knew was that the house had been in the man's family for many generations, but that it had been allowed to run into disuse recently, for reasons that were too vague to discover. As a result of that my family found itself starting on the trip of a lifetime, one that was expected to last many years. With it happening so quickly, I never had chance to realise what I was going to miss at home and by the time I landed it was too late and I was ready to embrace it with open arms. As things turned out, that 'many years' was only to last five glorious months.

Looking back, I can see that it was the most important period of my life, any young boy's dream. It was 1965 and anything was possible. It was an adventure beyond belief, one of exploration and personal development, and I would never reach its dizzying heights again. I was a cocky, spirited, ten-year old kid and this new world offered me plenty of excitement. In a way the whole problem started with me, but like most things in life you never quite realise what it all means at the time.

I had been exploring my new domain with all the gusto of those early Victorian explorers, blissfully unaware of the dangers, but well within the harsh restrictions my father had imposed on me—at least by my interpretation of them. I had decided that my first task was to explore the back garden. That was no mean feat in itself, because my Nigerian back garden was a bit different to my Yorkshire one. This one extended to the top of the mountain three thousand feet above us, so obviously I wasn't going to do it all in a day. My father had warned me not to get into trouble or wander too far away and so the bees became a welcome distraction.

I had noticed them within the first two days of my exploration. Eventually, I told my father about them, but that was after a few weeks investigating the strange phenomenon of those mysterious and fascinating insects. Now, for those of you who don't know, Nigerian Killer Bees are the size of small sparrows, well to a ten-year old kid they were, and they haven't diminished with the passage of time, quite the reverse if anything. They are mean, frightening looking things and I loved them at first sight. I noticed the first one about 100 yards from the back of the house, which, by then, was land covered by sparse brush. It caught my attention, because it was moving so slowly and on closer (though not too close) inspection, I realised it shouldn't have been flying at all. I couldn't work it out. It seemed to defy the laws of gravity. At first, I thought it was hovering in place, but it was simply that it was moving so slowly, as if every inch it gained was a struggle. The more I studied it the more convinced I became that it couldn't be flying, yet unless my eyes deceived me it clearly was.

It was a mystery I became determined to solve, but I wasn't stupid enough to try and capture one—they looked nasty. A vivid amber colour boldly stating 'hands off'. That first time I followed it for about five minutes before losing it. One minute it was there, I blinked and it was gone, which was crazy because, as I said, it moved so slowly. I took that as a personal affront. That it happened, time after time, over the next month or so, with infuriating regularity, drove me to distraction. Then I found out the reason why I had been losing sight of them. The sheer size of the thing had hidden it from me. What I had thought of as a tree was in fact the hive, although, I was sure somewhere under all that mass there was a tree. It had to be dead, though, because there was no sign of green shoots to show life that I could see. If the hive had killed it or the bees had simply taken over a dead tree, I had no way of knowing, but it was an incredible, haunting and beautiful sight.

The last time I had been so astonished by such a visual phenomenon was when I had gone on a school trip to York Minister. Obviously the hive was not as big, but it had that same aura about it and was just as awesome in its own unique way and all the more so, set in that spectacular background. The strange sounds of the other insects and birds, calling out their distress with my intrusion, under the African sky, a shade of blue that is unmatched anywhere else in the world. There was also a smell to the hive that was the mixture of sweetness and decay that was Nigeria, but far from unpleasant. I was entranced by its alien nature.

The ignorance of youth and a natural instinct for adventure had shielded me from any fear. As far as I was concerned the bees were just bees, albeit large ones. I didn't know how deadly they were until the day our cook left us. We had just finished saying grace when the cook dropped the serving dish, full of soup, with a clatter that was almost drowned out by her shrike. 'Mlumboh, Mlumboh,' she screamed and my father looked around, with a look of bewilderment, for the cause of her distress. Her face was screwed up as she stood amidst the spoiled soup, eyes fixed on the window, thankfully closed against the evening chill. I looked and saw three of my docile bees battering at the thin glass with a savage intent that surprised me. They looked much different to the lazy fat ones that I had spent so many hours chasing. Later, we found out that 'Mlumboh' was a local word that meant death. We never found that out from the cook though, because she had rushed from the room, packed her bags and left, despite everything my father said and ignoring all the questions my mother asked her. No amount of argument or inducement could change her mind.

We had a lot of trouble getting people to work for us after that incident because our home became known as the death house. It wasn't just that the Killer Bees were so deadly, although their sting was potent enough, rather it was because that in Nigeria bees are linked with death. The belief is that they are a link between life and death, they were messengers if you like, that travelled in both worlds. Also, at certain times of the year when the Harmattan Wind blows, they become very aggressive. While nobody understood why that was so, they all had a story to tell about their own narrow escape from them. I found out most of my information from old Jim, my friend. He lived in a shack on our property. I had found him there the first day I arrived at the house. Local rumour had it that he was over a hundred years old, he certainly looked it, but I wasn't so sure, because he had young eyes and an even younger mind. It didn't matter anyway; I would listen to his stories for hours on end. He had a rich dark voice and spoke better English than I did. He also had the gift of story telling, a talent that had a magic all of its own. One that held me captive. I would drink up the history of his world, which he brought to life for me with his rich vocabulary and his mimicry. I spent time with him as often as I possibly could. He had worked for the Mission all his life, and in some of his stories had even helped build it, but that was clearly impossible because the lintel stone had the date 1849 on it and he couldn't have been that old. I loved him all the same. He was the oldest person that I knew and in those days the older generation still commanded respect. He spoke with power and authority about the past and that gave his stories great credibility. His stories captivated me, even in those days when I couldn't sit still for a minute, in his presence, I did. I always left Jim feeling that I wanted to know more.

It was after the incident with the cook that I had told my father about the hive and he had forbidden me to go near it, after I'd taken him to see it of course. At the time, I thought that it was very unfair of him and sulked, but I did obey him. My father had then taken the problem to the local government man, Mr John, who promised the earth, but delivered nothing. It was after a frustrating two weeks or so that in desperation, my father took the issue to the local village elders, which, old Jim had said we should have done at the beginning. They told him that the Mission was cursed and only one man could help him. Dhurenni was a witch doctor by my fathers' standards and because of that my father was very reluctant to approach him. He didn't believe in all that 'mumbo jumbo nonsense' he repeated often enough. It was Sister Catherine who persuaded him to visit Dhurenni in the end. She pointed out that he wasn't really a witch doctor and that a literal translation of his title would be 'The King of the Bees.' In essence, she told him, Dhurenni was the expert, and to use him would not reflect on my fathers' beliefs, and that, coming from a Catholic nun, spoke volumes. He didn't look happy with what she said, but he did accept it.

Much to my surprise and delight, I was allowed to go with my father to the Ibo Village, Nguru, where Dhurenni lived. The village was in the northernmost part of Nigeria and was quite a long trip, especially in those pre-oil days, when the infrastructure was not up to much. I sat in the back of the old Wolsey we used over there, watching the beautiful landscape flow by, while I listened to my father talk about life with old Jim. Old Jim was related to Dhurenni by blood and that would make it difficult for Dhurenni to refuse us our request for his help. By the time we reached the village it was almost night. My father was worried about the long haul back in the dark, on roads that were little more than dirt tracks. As it turned out, however, that wasn't going to be a problem. We were to spend the night there, as the Chieftain's personal guests, which was an honour few outsiders were ever awarded in those days.

I was also allowed to attend the meeting of the Council of Elders that would listen to our request for help and then advise accordingly, but it was Dhurenni himself, who would make the final decision. Before all that, however, there was the food and celebration. I can't tell you what I ate and drank that night, and perhaps that's for the better by the appearance and smell of some of the dishes served, but the truth of it is, that it was the most delicious food I've ever tasted. Every mouthful seemed to erupt on my palette like ambrosia and it sent my senses reeling. I was caught up in the excitement, the newness of everything and intoxicated by the whole atmosphere. So much so that today, so many years later, separating fact from fiction is a task beyond me. Perhaps writing this down now is a form of therapy or, at the very least, a rationale of my madness.

My life was changed that night. No, I was changed by that night. I saw things that couldn't be, things that weren't and things that shouldn't be. At least according to everything that I knew to be truth prior to that night, or rather, by what I had been taught as the truth. Dhurenni was a witch doctor, a magician, a shaman, but, above all else, a showman beyond compare. At the height of his performance, he stood towering above me, twenty feet tall, chanting in 'Hausa'. His giant head changed before my startled eyes into a dark, writhing, living mask that came down closer and closer to me. Soon, so close that I could make out the individual Nigerian Killer Bees that made up the mask. They were crawling all over his face. I'm sure I screamed then for my father to help me as some of the bees came over to me and settled softly onto my skin and started to crawl over my terrified face. I was locked there, frozen and alone, without help, and I was scared. When the bees talked to me I was less surprised than I should have been. They asked me why I was scared and I was at a loss. I was stuck for an answer. I didn't know why I was scared of them, except that they were Nigerian Killer Bees. They told me that I hadn't been afraid of them when I had followed them to their hive. That was right and I never questioned how they knew that. I just wondered if my mind was playing tricks on me. How could they know what had happened over a hundred miles away? Still, if they were talking to me, why shouldn't they know? Maybe they could read my mind, because, as soon as I thought that they told me the answer to my unspoken question. *'What one bee knows, all bees know'*. That was the last thing I remember from that night, although I'm sure the celebrations went on much longer.

I woke up the following day during the drive home. I knew I was in the back of the car by the smell of the old leather and the bumpy ride. My father seemed in high spirits and while I drifted in and out of sleep I listened to him talk with Old Jim. In that half-asleep state I briefly wondered whose shoulder I rested on, but then, I knew it was Dhurenni.

·

With that knowledge came peace and sleep. I drifted off again into my fantastic dreams.

When we finally arrived back at the house my father asked Dhurenni in for a drink but he refused and said he would go to the hive straight away. 'I'll show you the way,' my father said and I held my breath, if he went, I couldn't.

'The King of the Bees can find his own way,' he replied in a quiet voice, but one that held great authority. I didn't ask my father if I could go with him, knowing instinctively that he wouldn't have approved. I soon caught up with Dhurenni and we walked together in comfortable silence to the hive.

When we arrived there, I knew what was expected of me without being told, but I don't know how I knew. I stood off to one side while Dhurenni approached the hive with a ceremonial air of precision that a regimental drill sergeant would have been proud of. He took short dancing steps around the hive until he had made a complete circuit. It was as if the night before I had made a bond with the bees. They had approved me and I had accepted them, and with that acceptance, knowledge came. Maybe, it was as simple as taking on faith something that was so unbelievable was real, I don't know, but as a result I understood what was going on.

My understanding of the ceremony that Dhurenni performed was in my head even though I had never experienced anything like it before. It was all over in a very short time. An offer was made to the bees. It was accepted and then the negotiations began. So simple in concept, yet so intricate in detail. If the bees would move, and the condition and deterioration of the hive suggested that was advisable soon, Dhurenni would find them a safe and acceptable alternative, one that would suit their needs better, and avoid further trouble with people. The details went on, but the bees' basic needs were small and it was as simple as that. However, it didn't end there, they had other news for us that was more important.

The bees bridge the gap between the two worlds of life and death and that gives them knowledge—and knowledge is power. They have the freedom to move with ease between both worlds. Of all the things of magic left in the world today, they are unique. Dhurenni was allowed to share some of their magic. He sat across the fire that we had made, and went into a trance, to walk his spirit in the bees' realm, with them as his guide and protector. In some way, the bond I now had allowed me to share this experience with him. I waited with patience while he remained in that state. When he returned, he told me about the great danger that was coming to his land. My family would have to leave because we would be targeted in the forthcoming struggle.

I wondered how I would be able to explain all this to my father as we walked back to the house. In the end it wasn't anything that I said. Many reports of the unrest were flooding in and the British High Commission ordered us to leave the country. The Civil War broke out within weeks of my family leaving Nigeria, and I worried about my new friends. I never went back to Nigeria although I kept in touch with what was going on there because soon after returning home I was allowed to have my own hive of bees and as you may remember, *'What one bee knows, all bees know.'*

King of the Bees © John Wrigglesworth 2000

'*May Day* is the lapel of a much darker suit—that suit being my novel, *This Is Oxford*,' **Clive Benger** tells us from Dartmoor. He says that his hunger for writing came after a woodland awakening where 'the woods screamed at me.' This is not the usual sort of background information we get from writers, but *May Day* is not the usual sort of story . . .

May Day (from *This is Oxford*)

Clive Benger

'...who in your merry merry month of May,
who by very slow decay ...' : L. Cohen

She knows full well how very much people enjoy books. They come home to their partners from the workplaces and they eat supper. Together they watch the six o'clock Evening News, and the evening slips by. They slip in and out of a hot bath and then into bed, where they slip into the books that they are reading, and finally into sleep.

She remembers those simple times—how the reliable vehicle of a book could transport her from things on the news. She remembers cocoa at bedtime; cocoa made with scalded milk and mixed with honey; thyme bee honey from Greece; the Grecian thyme fields, 'far as the eye could see', freckled sporadically with white hives, while the sirocco air seethes with warmth. And she remembers, 'Goodnight love.'

The honey jar is washed out now and it is a container for pretty coloured beads among buttons that have come off. The evening news is even more full of unsafe things and there is no more, 'Goodnight love.'

At least she has the books. She very much enjoys reading the books.

'Rowan?' said Stephen gently.

She tugged herself upright in the dining chair and turned over her open book. It looked like a pagoda roof lying there on the faded varnish of the table. She sighed. She must have nodded off again into a reverie.

'Rowan, what you are feeling, what you are going through, it's only natural.' And he pulled up a chair and sat close to her. It seemed to him that she had not heard.

'Rowan?'

'Morning Stephen,' she tried to smile, but it was stillborn on her lips.

'Rowan, what you are feeling is . . . ' She clipped him.

'Only natural, yes I heard you.'

They sat in deafening silence for a few painful moments.

'I'm sorry,' said Rowan. 'I snapped at you.'

'That's okay,' he said.

Her brow pinched and she balled her fists up, saying, 'If this is supposed to be bloody natural then why does it feel so bloody unnatural? It's crazying me Stephen, it's crazying me!'

She flung herself down across the table, knocking the book flying and she just lay there. He chewed his lip.

'The unnaturality,' he said, 'If there is such a word, well . . . it's only natural,' he assured her. He wanted to say more. His eyes rolled left to look into his creative side for something more to offer. Finding no inspiration there he just turned his focus directly on to her.

'This won't be easy,' he said, 'because it isn't easy ... but Joanna and I, well . . . we would like you to get some counselling.'

Rowan started slightly in her chest. An outward tic barely registered but it was there so she felt damaged.

'I don't want to go out Stephen,' she said to the table.

'You think perhaps . . . maybe we didn't notice this,' he stated calmly. 'You've been here three weeks now and you haven't even been out into the garden.'

She shrugged, felt hassled and ran her fingers through her hair as if her head hurt.

'This is Oxford,' Stephen said, like it meant something. It provoked her. The isolation that Rowan had loved at Sancreed . . . home . . . she subsequently came to hate. She loathed the entire area of Penwith eventually. 'Go out shopping,' people had advised her. The nearest shops were four miles away. They were Penzance. Penzance had become a loaded gun of memories with which she blew her brains out every day. In the end every blade of waving grass in Penwith represented a headstone erected 'In Loving Memory'. And the rookery in the garden of the house just sounded like traffic skidding on tarmac. Oxford would afford new distraction. She had friends there. Oxford would be full of life, where Sancreed was something else. In Oxford now she felt that it would be wrong to give herself so freely to its many distractions. She had been here for almost three weeks and had remained in the house; she was in a state of mental impasse. Could not go out. Could not go forward. Maybe she did need counselling.

'No . . no . . Stephen, not counselling,' she said. 'Not anything to do with . . . It . . . .'

Stephen breathed out.

'Okay Rowan, I understand.' Lately, whenever he was talking with her, waiting for an answer, he found himself holding his breath for ages.

'Maybe something else instead,' he said and sucked in a lungful of air.

'Yes, maybe.'

'You know,' he said, 'there's Hinksey Park only a minute's walk from here.'

'Park?' She seemed genuinely interested to hear this, and not just trying to please him. Her posture uncoiled and relaxed a little. She stopped looking at the table and she looked at Stephen. He noticed her eyes change. They turned softer, and more focused. He felt softer and more focused too.

'Yes,' he enthused, 'Hinksey Park. It's got pedalo boats, an adventure playground, there's a big lake and some swans live there...'

'Swans?' she clipped him again.

'Yes, swans. A pair of them with plucky cygnets and there are all sorts of trees there as well. I saw a fox once, and there was this one time, I even saw a kingfisher.'

'Kingfishers are amazing aren't they,' Rowan joined in. Stephen was glowing like a lovely young boy.

'Yes they are. It's only a minute's walk to get to Hinksey Park,' he said. 'It's so pretty there.'

He went and fetched Rowan's fleece jacket, but when he offered it to her she shrank from it.

'It's a beautiful fleece jacket,' he said dangling it at her from his outstretched hand. 'Please put it on and come to the park with me. I'd really like your company. Come Rowan.'

She took the fleece jacket from him and put it on.

'Okay Stephen,' she said, 'let's go out.'

It was 1 May 2000.

The time spent together in Hinksey Park began with a solemn silence. Rowan's smiles were like buses, none for ages, then three double-deckers would come at once.

Stephen made a point of not talking, but pointed at things and let her do the talking if she liked. And she did like, too. She began many small conversations with soft enthusiasm, and he encouraged her with nods, smiles and smaller talk and enjoyed watching her emerge from her gloom. He pointed to a patch of purple delicate looking flowers.

'It's like a ginormous duvet!' Rowan squealed, and ran fast to them, like an infant girl, but stopped just short of the quilt of flowers so as not to crush a one.

'What are these odd little flowers?' Rowan asked as Stephen caught her up. 'They are so beautiful and strange. They look like they're made out of shards of a snakeskin, but they're not sort of crispy, they're perfectly silken.'

Rowan put a lilting cadence into her words, which in a musical way was asking Stephen if he could understand her imagery. She looked at him to see if he understood.

'I know exactly what you mean,' he smiled. 'They're called, Snakes Head Fritillaries in fact. Didn't you have any in Sancreed?'

'I've never seen any before,' she said, and knelt down for a closer inspection of the detail of the flowers.

'Fritillaries. Splendid, lovely name for such beautiful, amazing flowers,' she said. Then she squinted up at Stephen and asked, 'May I pick one?'

'They're quite rare actually,' he said and worriedly chewed his bottom lip.

She bit her own lip, 'Just one. I'd keep it pressed in my book.' She produced a little blue note book from her fleece jacket pocket.

He couldn't condone it, nor simply say, no. 'They're rare,' he said. Rowan still chewing at her lip picked a good one.

'Sorry,' she said not looking up at him and secreted the flower into the little book.

'You are full of rebellions!' Stephen gasped.

'Oh, but those rebellions are not mine,' she said, and rolled her eyes mischievously.

'Not your rebellions,' he said, not asking, but wanting her to go on. 'They belong to him,' she said and prodded her chest. 'Him who?'

'The Wolf,' she stood up and marched away fast to an oak tree. She leaned against it and surveyed the ripples on the big lake for swans. Stephen followed her at a smart pace.

'The Wolf has rebellions, I see,' he said, not really seeing.

Not taking her eyes off the lake, Rowan asked, 'What's your animal, Stephen?' Her voice was like witchcraft.

Stephen shrugged, 'Animal?' he said.

'At Sancreed, home, we had a four day workshop once to discover our animal spirit allies,' she said. 'It turns out I am a *he* wolf, alpha male, The Wolf,' Rowan was proud seeming, swollen with it, and her breathing had become hard, almost panting, and her eyes glistened.

'This is fascinating!' Stephen said.

'I can already guess what your animal spirit ally is, but I can't tell it to you,' she said. 'That wouldn't be proper. You'll have to let me lead you on a guided visualisation so you and your ally can meet,' she explained. 'Then you'll know.'

Stephen had become completely enthralled at what Rowan was talking about. He wanted an animal spirit ally that instant.

It would be great. It would enhance him as a man and might even complete him as a person. He became awash with some of the benefits it would yield. All his own idiosyncrasies and personal rebellions could be vindicated by this new dynamic in his psyche. When Joanna had caught him having that party-snog with Lucy he could have blamed it on his 'stag within, rutting'. Okay that might sound extreme, but it seemed to him that the possibilities might be endless.

'I want this!' he said. 'It's amazing. Take me on this . . . this . . . what *did* you call it?'

'Guided visualisation.'

'Yes, that. Take me on it now.'

'Can't,' she said, and dropped her eyes off the lake and on to her feet, and then askance to him. 'Can't yet, Stephen. I'm a bit too blind to do visualisations just lately.' She had been swallowed up again into the gloom suddenly.

'Of course,' he understood.

Hinksey Park had created a temporary veil of illusion over Rowan's dark mood and had made her brighten, but that iridescence waxed and waned and the illusion was gone—as though a night cloud

had covered the full shine of the moon. Stephen had been enchanted by the park and Rowan, and how easily he had forgotten the point of coming here, but noticed now how it had worked for a while. Being reminded of Rowan's sadness he gravitated back to it. He met her eye noting how it had darkened again with renewed glumness. Feeling guilty for bringing the mood down she gave Stephen bursts of weak smiles. But they stood in stark silence.

'I thought Oxford was all dreaming spires . . . well I haven't seen one yet,' Rowan said, twirling away from the oak tree with a push, and quickly walked off. Stephen found himself having to speed again to catch her up.

'I'll show you spires,' he said when he caught her.

'No,' she said, 'I'm out here now, so you've done your bit. My wolf can take a turn at *loco parentis*.'

He stopped walking, stunned, but she paced on.

'Rowan, I don't want you to go to town on your own, it just doesn't seem a good idea.'

'I'll be fine,' she called out without stopping or looking back. Stephen felt stuck.

'But this is Oxford,' he said.

'Go home,' Rowan shouted. 'Joanna might be up now. Go back home.'

He could only stand and watch as Rowan crossed the cricket green, and turning left onto Abingdon Road, she exited the park.

The Oxford University Press building threw a monumental shadow across Walton Street as it basked in the Jericho sun at noon. In the aorta of the company, Fin swivelled round from his screen in English Dictionary, stood up, stretched, and rubbed his eyes.

'Judy, I'm going to lunch now,' he yawned.

Judy sat back, curled a slender white arm behind her head, and played with her blond scut of hair. She tried to suppress a yawn, but the one that Fin had done was too infectious.

'How long do you reckon you'll be?' she asked.

"Bout an hour,' he replied over his shoulder as he left the office. He came out of the building into the shade of its Walton Street courtyard, and he lingered alone by the fountain. The ducks with their ducklings that made such a fun sight in the fountain ignored Fin as he watched them at their antics. The Mallard Drake repeatedly upended and righted himself in front of the fluffy young ones. Fin, given to comedy, translated the quacks that he heard into English.

'Now then children that was a 'duck-dive' and notice carefully please how the water just runs off my back. That part is very important, and is a thing that, as ducks, we are very proud of.' Chuckling at his own wit, Fin turned left out of the courtyard and on to Walton Street.

He was wondering whether to cross the road now and have lunch at Freud's, or whether to go up this side to the pedestrian crossing outside the piano shop and cross over and have lunch at the Jericho Cafe instead. It was in this quandary that he discovered that he had absent-mindedly, carelessly, already put himself on to the road. A Tetley's Bitter dray lorry bore down on him with ferocious speed, its air horn hollering and its mighty wheels locking up. He stood frozen to the road while the heat of the engine was all over him, but did nothing to thaw him sufficiently to move. Only his arms moved. They threw up and covered his face. 'I'm going to die!' he thought.

Fin was solidly impacted and he flew up from the road. His knuckles, his smooth face and his shorn head scraped along the pavement. His arms and his legs were at rag-doll angles. The shrieking tyres died and the horn stopped breathing. Finally Fin stopped moving, and he lay still. Consciousness was leaking away from him. Voices seemed to come from everywhere.

'Did I hit him? Oh God, did I hit him?'
'I think you hit him. Did anyone see this?'
'I didn't mean to hit him ... He just stepped out.'
'You hit him square, man!'
'God, no.'
'Did you see this?'
'Saw him flyin', man, he's dead.'
'No, God, no.'
'He never hit him.'
'What?'
'I thought I saw a girl hit him.'
'The dude is dead man!'
'Please, God, no.'

'I saw a girl. Where's the girl?'

'God, no.'

A huge aeroplane passed low overhead on its way to land at Kidlington Airport, and no one could hear a thing for a while. Couldn't even think.

Galloway sat outside The Bodleian Library, soaking up the May Day sun, and nursing his May Day hangover. What with all the partying, he hadn't slept in two days, and didn't want to go home to sleep now. He was on a mission. A May Day mission. What's it all about? Though his brain felt stale he could well remember the celebrations this morning, and the memory of the street musicians was still fresh. There had to be a reason for this annual revelry. He'd loved all the different music he'd heard when he came up the High Street earlier. There were didgeridoos, flutes, lutes, guitars, bongo drums and bells. The sound was utterly bewitching as it resounded off the ancient colleges of Magdalen, University and Queens. There had to be morris dancers too.

'Do you do this dancing every May Day?' Galloway had asked a be-belled and be-batoned man in a hat of fresh flowers.

'If we did not, there'd be no crop this annum from Wytham Woods to Whitnam Clumps, nor Islip to Shotover,' the man said as he adorned his bushy beard with daisies.

'Really?' asked Galloway, who was so stewed on Bacchanalia that he was really falling for these folklores.

'Really,' said the Morris dancer who noticed that by the glaze on Galloway's eye he was believing in the superstitions and rites. 'We dance to bless the fields and to ward off evil. You know evil when you see it, do you, lad?'

'I don't know,' said Galloway.

'Don't know! You must be beggin' to lose your soul lad. Beware the witches and fairy maidens today boy.'

Galloway wandered off and bought a sprig of heather from a gypsy woman and received her Romany blessing.

'Heather's for luck, blessin's for protection. It's a square and round love,' said the gypsy and held out her bony hand.

'Square and round?' asked Galloway.

'That's a pound, love,' explained the woman.

He spent some quiet time in the public library next to The Westgate Centre and researched this peculiar tradition of May Day in Oxford. But it revealed nothing except that the choirboys of Magdalen College sang madrigals at 6.00 a.m. on this day atop the Magdalen Tower. It never said why. A librarian suggested that Galloway should continue his research at the more prestigious Bodleian Library in Radcliffe Square. He was feeling only a bit undone when it transpired that only members of the Student Union were allowed in there.

So it came to pass that he was sat on the bleached steps of The Bodleian Library and was looking directly at Blackwell's Bookshop, across Broad Street, opposite. Blackwell's was busy on this warm day. People were to-ing and fro-ing there, like thoughts in a head.

'Lorelei!' he suddenly gasped.

She came out of Blackwell's clutching a little bag that bore the same name upon it, and the volume in the bag indicated she had just purchased a book. Her jeans were like a dirty blue second skin. Her t-shirt was tight and vastly swollen, and the faded love heart print that was taut across the mammoth twin swellings was a hypnotic focal point. Her burnished copper hair hung in greasy stranglets that tangled down, pooled over her shoulders and cascaded below her bottom—it was hair that seemed an impossible length and impossible colour. The girl had slightly parted bee-stung lips, and a dear little nose that turned up ever such a tiny bit and looked winsome. Her nose and her Irish looking cheeks were smattered with the most charming show of freckles. Her eyes looked like drops of melted plain chocolate, and she looked fit to burst into floods of tears at any moment. Her beauty was beyond human. Galloway thought of imps, nymphs, sirens and faeries. Already his soul seemed to be flying out of his weary body.

'Lorelei,' he muttered, and creaked up on to his aching feet to follow this charm.

Dragging her lovely blue fleece jacket behind her in the dust of Broad Street with a new reading book in a little Blackwell's bag, Rowan had no idea that she was being followed. She found a safe place to get across St. Giles and while she waited for the red man to turn into the green man outside Boswell's, she secretly hated seeing other pedestrians making a dash for it in front of buses and taxis. She followed her senses, which led her down George Street, past the Apollo Theatre where 'Oklahoma' was billed. Further down, the MGM cinema was now showing 'Beyond Rangoon' and a little way on from there she bought a cold Beck's beer in The Old Fire Station for refreshment.

There is a full size model of the lower half of a fireman sliding down a pole, through the ceiling, into the bar. Rowan smiled at this nice touch.

She had seen dreaming spires now. She had paid a pound in St Mary's Church on the High Street, and climbed up to the tower where she was rewarded with the breath-taking panorama of all of Oxford. The intricate and loving detail on the gargoyles filled her with warmth and a sense of fun. The round building of the Radcliffe Camera was a treat to look upon from the dizzy heights of the tower. People on the street below looked like soot and dust being blown by the wind.

Rowan finished drinking her Becks beer out of the bottle. She stuck her pointed tongue into its green neck to get one last taste from it, and then she burped. Galloway observed this in the mirrors behind the bar . . and was completely certain she was a demon of May Day out to snare men's souls. He resumed tailing her when she left out through the back doors and mixed in with the throng off Gloucester Green market. He almost lost her as she slipped up Friars Entry, but she lingered outside The Gloucester Arms. Rock music was blaring out of there. He heard the words of the song being played, 'Hell ain't a bad place to be,' and he chilled. Rowan shook her hair around for a moment, to the music before skipping gaily up the alleyway and turning out on to the join of St. Giles into Woodstock Road.

Little Clarendon Street, just off of the start of Woodstock Road, has a continental allure about it. The shops are all 'gift shoppie' and the eateries all have mini extensions that spill out on to the pavement. It smells richly of foods from around the globe and at regular intervals across the cobbled street are stretches of coloured light bulbs. At night it is like a carnival. In the daytime it is simply Christmas always.

Rowan was magnetised into the first shop there called 'Animal-Animal'. She handled all of the wolf merchandise with utter glee, but eventually bought a little bean bag llama. Through the window she saw a young man staring at her and she wondered if she had seen those same tired, furtive eyes before. Perhaps in the Old Fire Station? She thought little of it as her tummy occupied her mind now.

Two shops down she looked at the George and Davis Café.

'Let's get a coffee and a burger here,' said an American to another American as they pushed past her.

'*Yeah, The Mad Cow Cafe, Great. Order me a double Latte and a bagel.*'

Rowan rain-checked it because she was not into doughnut worship. Michael's Brasserie looked seductive on the outside, but she couldn't see through the windows at the interior so she never went in there. The Bar-Celona looked great for an evening, but was empty now.

The Dom looked too fashion conscious rather than cuisine conscious. By now Rowan was really flaking with hunger. Galloway was certain the witch was looking for a man to seduce. She was growing weary for looking and frustrated because her time left in the human realm was short. He really believed this.

At last on Walton Street, Rowan settled on Freud's for lunch. It was a beautiful and very, very old church that had long been renovated as a fashionable eatery and jazz club. She flounced up its steps and dropped into a plastic chair under the shade of a parasol.

'Hi, can I get you a menu, or would you just like something to drink?' asked a pretty waitress with a sonorous Austrian accent.

'Oh, thank you, may we have a pitcher of water with ice, and do you have a Becks beer?' asked Rowan.

'Sure, you want one?'

'Yes please, and a pizza would be great.'

'Seafood pizza, Hawaiian, Three cheese...' suggested the waitress.

'Just a big one with pepperoni and that stringy cheese,' said Rowan.

'Mozzarella?'

'Yeah, that, please.'

'It's coming right up.'

Just then Galloway came up the steps looking like a crazed man, and he dumped his sweaty, fatigued body into another plastic chair at a different table.

'Be right with you,' said the waitress to him. He nodded and extended his parasol open. But it was defunct, and would not obey his shaking hands. The Jericho sun beat down and he looked at Rowan, he felt cursed.

'She's put a hex on me,' he thought. 'She knows I know she's a demon.' He felt certain of all this, and continued working in vain with the parasol.

'Are you alright?' asked Rowan. She could see the guy was almost delirious. 'Do you want to share my table? The parasol works,' she asked and she recognised that he was the guy she'd seen through the window of Animal-Animal. He had been in The Old Fire Station too.

'No,' he declined earnestly. 'No . . . I'm just fine here. No worries.'

'You can come over here if you like, I don't bite,' she said showing her bright teeth to him.

He shook his head. 'She knows I know,' was all that he could think.

Her food and drink came and she fell upon it hungrily. Galloway suddenly thought of a jackal at a carcass on the Serengeti Plain. When Rowan's blood sugar was up and the pizza was entirely finished, she licked the plate clean and burped. Galloway didn't expect anything more than this lack of decorum from a May Day demon. 'She may look more beautiful than is humanly possible but her mind and its ambitions are unnaturally ugly,' he realised.

'Lorelei,' he muttered.

The waitress came outside and gave Rowan her bill, and then turned to go.

'Oh, don't go,' said Rowan. 'I'll settle up now ... What is it? Eight-fifty? Here's a ten, keep it.'

'Thank you very much, that's really...' but the voice of the waitress faded away from Rowan's concentration. Rowan could not believe what was happening on the other side of the road. Her face became completely drained.

'That's my man,' she said and tears pierced her eyes.

'Pardon me?' said the waitress.

'He's . . . he should be . . . It's him over there!' Rowan mumbled and tears were just running down her face, but she wasn't sobbing at all. She got to her feet and, shaking, went down the steps.

'That girl is possessed,' said Galloway to the waitress. 'I've been following her.'

Ignoring Galloway, the waitress called out, 'Miss, are you okay?' But Rowan never heard her. She had stepped out on to the road. Her eyes were fixed across it. The waitress saw a handsome young man had also stepped out into the road, and he looked confused.

Rowan was running now, and a Tetley's Bitter lorry was launching at the man. Impact suddenly was a fact of life. The reality of this now unavoidable tragedy was almost comical. A small hysteric slipped out of the waitress's mouth . . . and died. The guy would be killed. That was a fact, and the girl running at him, she would be killed too. The waitress's eyes were wide now waiting for the scene to play out to its bloody end.

The horn was shrieking, tyres were biting tarmac and sounded like a rookery at dawn. But Rowan got to the man before the lorry did. She used her entire body to punch him away, and then she herself fell flat to the road as the lorry passed harmlessly over her and seized still at last.

'This is amazing!' said the waitress running down the steps to the gathering crowd of voices.

Both now in the John Radcliffe hospital, Rowan took two plastic cups of vending machine cocoa into Fin's private room. They had to stay in overnight. They were both pretty exhausted.

She passed Fin a cocoa and from her dressing gown pocket took out a new novel that she'd bought today.

'I thought we could read a story together,' she said.

'Yeah, slide up here next to me,' said Fin. 'What book is it?'

'*Grimm Tales*, it's fairy stories.'

'I enjoy reading books,' said Fin. And when he finished reading *Hansel and Gretel* to Rowan, he realised she was already fast asleep. 'Goodnight love,' he whispered to the girl who saved his life today.

May Day (from *This is Oxford*) © Clive Benger 2000

Museums of crime and punishment have become popular tourist attractions in recent years. The London Dungeon attracts vast numbers of people who pay good money to enjoy the simulated experience of old-fashioned incarceration and torture, while the Nottingham Galleries of Justice is reckoned to be one of the most comprehensive collections of the genre. Other perhaps more authentic museums—in that they are situated in prison buildings—include the Clerkenwell House of Detention, Kings Lynn's Old Gaol House, Kilmainham Gaol in Dublin and Inverary Jail Museum in Scotland. And then there is Bodmin Gaol in Cornwall. PWI received this account of one of the less commercialised prison museums from **Bill Hook,** a passing visitor and holiday penologist.

The Ballad of Bodmin Jail

Bill Hook

I have always enjoyed spotting things with a potential for cult status. You know the kind of thing: Trebants, apostrophes, the *Royston Crow* (which, believe it or not, is a newspaper in Cambridgeshire), The Outer Space Act 1986 (yes, it does exist), Shàg Connor and the Carrot Crunchers. I could go on for days. Bodmin Jail slipped into my Top Twenty at around number 16, but each time I go there things seem yet more bizarre, so that it is rising rapidly and could soon reach number one, if not pipped to the post by the Millennium Dome. The jail represents a lost world—but it is well worth the pilgrimage if you are ever passing that way, if only to understand the difference between enthusiasm for an idea and delivery of the product. 'All men kill the thing they love', as Oscar Wilde remarked.

Like Oxford prison (now being reborn, among other things, as a shopping mall) and the London Dungeon (now the London Dungeon), Bodmin ended its working life some years ago. But in an age when developers were not so inclined to snap up such places with one eye on the accommodation needs of nouveau riche computer geeks, it became a tourist attraction—and this is where the cult bit comes in. Bodmin was never given a makeover. Indeed, it is so dilapidated, so run-down, and seemingly bought and run on a shoestring. If ever a prison was a place of despair this crumbling stone edifice on the edge of town, crudely secured with a token strand of barbed wire (to stop people getting in over the wall?), is it.

Bodmin jail lost touch with reality long ago, I think—over ten years ago at least, which was when I first visited the place, thinking that here I would get a sense of what it must have been like for a West Country felon in former times. It was in the same chaotic state then and each of my two follow up inspections (forgive me if I have ideas above my station) has confirmed that both the jail and everything within it are lost in a charming time warp, untouched by modernization, investment or renovation and resistant to any form of takeover which might lead to the place being tidied up or to the installation of a MacDonalds. No stylish ticket booth with a computer to generate future unsolicited mail, no hint of strategic planning, and no sign on the horizon of, say, a Virtual Reality Prison Experience Centre. Just a sense of living from hand to mouth (the proprietors as well as the stuffed inmates): what might have been the flagship of the Pretend Prison Service overseen by a man in a makeshift outfit, ushering visitors along after the manner of Basil Fawlty. 'This way for the cellars. Come along there, madam . . . haven't got all day . . . Please don't mention Tasmania.'

Once inside, fresh sensations flood over the visitor like rain in a drought—and the mind is exercised by mischievous questions: 'Is this where you keep the coal, or is it a cell?'; 'Did the backlighting come from British Home Stores?'; 'How do they know that everyone has come out at the end of the day?' (such are the recesses, blind corners and opportunities for blending in with the scenery). Deep within each coal bunker, eerie scenes of reflection and remorse are depicted and one is tempted to add bubbles over the heads of the models—most of which look as if they were rounded up on Guy Fawkes night and persuaded they would be more at home living in an establishment which is a tribute Blue Peter and sticky-back-plastic. 'This treadmill was the making of me'; 'I owe it all to the cat o'nine tails and that chap in the black mask'. 'When I get out I'm going to take up oakum picking full-time'. Any overcrowding at Bodmin appears to be due not to an increase in crime but to some department store selling off its mannequins.

As one example of many tributes to missed opportunity, the really interesting parts of the jail—the architecture, decaying wings, the real cells and landings, the main courtyard and even the execution shed—are all accessible from the road without payment. Here, the passer-by can stand in wonderment within cavernous, cathedral like shells of buildings and gaze skywards through the landings and what remains of the roof. Among the mud, dankness and decay it is possible to visualise the five hundred or so men and women who once shared the place with rats and other vermin. What meagre food were prisoners of those times fed, and how, in days before electricity did they survive the sense of isolation and powerlessness as the mist descended and the truly classic iron doors, still in their original position (if somewhat rusted), were closed on them?

Likewise, there is free access to the gallows, where anyone can just wander in off the highway and fiddle with the levers. However, here the authenticity of the unretouched parts of the jail again evaporates and the make believe pit falls unscientifically short of the Home Office 'Table of

Drops', leaving yet another awkward question for the tour guide when he re-appears from serving the ice-creams. 'Excuse me, Mr. Fawlty, but did they kill Cornish felons by breaking their knees . . . and is it true that one chap hit the ground running and made off over the gate?'

By Herculean effort, the highly committed proprietors have constructed from newspapers the stories of all the 55 people executed at Bodmin. When I asked to see these dog-eared, but massively interesting broadsheets they were retrieved from behind the bar complete with ashtray-cum-paperweight and handed to me only after a thorough beating against the wall. I am no forensic expert, but they seem to have been created on an old Underwood typewriter operated with uncertain touch. If so, that could be the most valuable item in the place and the owners might be well advised to contact the Scott Fitzgerald Museum.

These records disclose that in former days—in what seems to have been an early gesture in the direction of liberal reform—executions at Bodmin were timed for after lunch, the idea being that the London mail coach might arrive with a reprieve. On occasion the mail was late and the arrangements were delayed until it did get there. What a dreadful place to be executed, if one had a choice, and the thought of the condemned man or woman (several women were executed at Bodmin) gibbering, shaking and straining his or her ears for the post horn beggars belief.

Bodmin is indeed the Fawlty Towers of prisons and it is easy to picture the Governor behind his desk (The Governor's House built into the wall of the prison has become a des res) signing orders and instructions and hoping the mail from London never would arrived. With minimum assistance, he could continue to perform all roles: on the gate, behind the counter, in the kitchens (literally everything on the meagre menu was '. . . off today, I'm afraid'), as commissionaire and as giftshop keeper—so as to ensure that visitors leave with the statutory T-Shirt ('I've been to Bodmin Jail'), pamphlet and car sticker. Fully in keeping, the souvenir shop is based on the Oxfam model and situated in an oversize room, lined with trestle tables covered in plastic memorabilia of the 'everything for a pound' variety, and with enough space for a game of badminton in the middle.

No doubt he would also wish to run the officers' mess, now a pub. Here one can join the locals and drink away one's penological cares whilst being cured in tobacco smoke so thick that it rises to the ceiling, condenses on impact and trickles down the walls fully distilled. I suspect he would also wish to remain in charge of the spare heads, arms, legs and other body parts visible to all and sundry in the garage.

The Ballad of Bodmin Jail © Bill Hook 2000

Postcsript: As PW went to press it was reported in the national media that Bodmin Jail is up for sale, the owners having apparently 'given up the ghost' after almost 20 years, the earlier part of which, it is also reported, they survived by living in the prison.

Robert Francis Mone was born in Scotland but spent his formative years in London. Presently in HMP Shotts, Lanarkshire, he is serving a life sentence.

Poems by Robert Francis Mone

Today

Today I sent a letter
It contained

All my hopes
All my fears
All my plans
All my tears

All my fevered frequent cries
For a glimpse of something better

Today I launched a paper boat
It carried

All my life
All my love
All my words
All my hurt

All that I so craved
As I struggled to stay afloat

Today I flew a paper plane
It bore away

All my thoughts
All my dread
All my dreams
All I've said

All that I have ever claimed
I would never do again

Today

Memories

The rockery grew easy
As I forked it day by day
Lifting out the memories
Until all was stripped and grey

Each piece of rooted wilderness
Prised from where it lay
Rudely on the naked earth
I lavished all my day

On plants so single-mindedly
Made pure and perfect form
Their rich and loamous territory
Once wild and overgrown

Some placed there quite deliberately
Some chance upon the wind
But tightly interwoven
In a life I would rescind

I tug so hard to break them free
And some do sever whole
But tendrils always linger
In the corners of my soul

Seasons Of the Heart

Here I sit and the earth is wrapped in snow
And the cold air is thick with falling night

I think of the still, dewy summer eves
When the cows come sauntering up sweet Cherry Lane
Waiting to nibble at juicy grass

When the green, green earth was full of changing life
When the warm wind blew softly, slowly past
Caressing now and then some wayside flower
Stopping to stir the tender aspen leaves
And breathing all its fragrance on the air

I think of the broad meadows so daisy white
With the long shade of some stray apple tree
Falling across them, and the rustlings faint
When evening breezes shook along the grass

I think of all the summer sounds
The cricket's chirp repeated near and far
The sleepy note of robins in their nest,
The jet dole crow whose sudden cry rang out
Plaintive yet strong, upon the startled air

And so it was the summer twilight fell
And deepened to the darkness of the night
And now I lift my heart out of the dream
And see instead the pale cold and dying lights,
The dull grey skies and barren snow clad fields
That come to us when loveless evenings fall

Juxtaposition

An innocent juxtaposition
as you move on the stair
making an image
the artist never foresaw

Two strangers who meet
in the holding of eyes
make a shrine of this place

An afternoon sun at the window
and stillness, a further dimension
haunting the gallery we dream in

With each movement we pose
another question outside the frame

And fill the space between
the artist and the moment
with the silence of lovers

Kensington 1965

In this quiet room
lives have been measured
by the movement of words
Across the silence our fingers touch
and time slows itself
to the turning of leaves
Say to me
'Good morning, Bobby',
for I am tired
and alone as a magpie
that has lost its mate

I pace the floor
sipping warm chablet,
pick up books
and just as easily
drop them to the table,
like so many unwanted twigs
or meaningless nights

Clouds brood low
over the city
as I stand by the river of my dreams
watching the water
turn to the colour of your eyes

Your image, a late autumn bird,
tries to flit by
but at the first flurry
of the feathery wing beat
I turn and my mind holds you,
cherishing your dusky lightness
till some emptily dead thing
forces the cage door, and
you ripple away,
lost in your dark and ancient land

Searching

Even though I know
you are not here
I search for you

Even though I know
you are not coming,
I wait for you

Sometimes I feel strong
with my patience
and eternal hope

Sometimes I feel weak
with my despair
and fruitless love

When people define things
differently,
honesty is not the same
as truth

From Future to Past

From Future to Past

Clare Barstow was inspired to write *Winding Back* after reading a collection of Will Self stories in which he 'plays with the conceived notions of time and space, turning the traditional ideas of story telling inside out.' She is currently working on the possibility of developing it into a novel. A lifer in Cookham Wood, Clare became a regular contributor to *Prison Writing* soon after it began. A committed writer of fiction, prose, poetry and drama, she has won 31 Koestler Awards. One of her plays went to the Edinburgh Festival in 1997 and several others have been performed in different prisons. 'Writing,' she says, 'has enabled me to cope more easily with all the traumas of prison life and has given me new-found inspiration in other areas of creativity.'

Winding Back

Clare Barstow

My name is Billy Haylett. It's not a real name in the conventional sense but then I was never formally given one nor did I inherit it. In fact my whole life thus far has been marked by an altered reality and I am constantly filled with the sensation of pushing against the tide. My story is one of strange reversal and starts where most people's end—or does it? Perhaps you are a better judge than I am as an outside observer always is.

My earliest memory is one of waking up in a park on a grass bank. At the time I had no conception of where I was or who I was or what I was. At first I saw only hazy shapes and shades but gradually my eyes adjusted to the light. I must have looked baffled as a woman came up to me and spoke to me. I have no recollection of what she said and indeed had no understanding of any language at that time. I tried desperately to emulate her but could only make a grunting sound, which caused her to run away. I saw her in the distance gesticulating to a park keeper and pointing in my direction. He also came up to me and attempted to communicate but I could only grunt again and flailed my arms wildly when he endeavoured to touch me. The woman was appointed to guard over me while he went off to contact the police.

I was obviously very disturbed, as I had no perception of what was taking place but only learnt the true facts later. Apparently he thought I was drunk and when two police officers arrived they also supposed the same and were forced to carry me between them to the car, as I could not comprehend the physical aspect of propulsion. I was taken to the station where more people attempted to examine me. A doctor adjudged that I was not drunk but suffering from a medical condition or had severe brain damage.

After several hours locked in a damp smelly cell, an ambulance arrived and took me to a hospital, which I now know was the Royal Free in Hampstead. Here I underwent a series of tests whereby no severe brain damage was discovered but expert opinion concluded I had some form of senile dementia. I was totally helpless and could not carry out the simplest task. They put me in a private room for fear that I would alarm the other patients. My age was proscribed to be 75 and my natural curiosity at my surroundings led me to be labelled by some as a simple pervert. Yet I had no conception of what was normal and therefore could not consciously divert from it. The basics of eating, bathing and even sitting were alien to me and it took me several weeks to master the rudimentary aspects of these.

I was regarded by most of the professionals as something of a freak, particularly as for the first weeks I was chained to the bed to prevent me from falling out and hurting myself. To some I was an interesting case but even they grew tired of me when I failed to always make the expected progress.

After three months I was transferred to the care of the local authorities who promptly put me in a specialist clinic treated the ailments of the elderly. I was to be given 24-hour supervision at first. I was still pretty inarticulate but could communicate any most basic needs by pointing to the relevant area that required attention. When they were not met immediately I became impatient and am ashamed to say that I often got out of control. I had no sense of morality nor could I grasp the bare essentials of the codes of human behaviour. For one year I stayed in my room as my carers felt I could not mix with the other patients. Fortunately there was a young psychologist there called Sophie who was quite sympathetic and could tolerate my idiosyncrasies more than the others. One day I saw her staring at pieces of paper whilst sitting with me and I demanded to know what was taking up her attention. I pushed her until she comprehended that I was curious about her reading.

Slowly over the weeks and months she attempted to teach me how to talk and read in addition to learning to walk. My first attempts at talking were largely inarticulate but by slowly repeating the letters of the alphabet and looking at their translation onto paper I was able to make some level of progress. Sophie would smile and look happy if I had done well which was encouragement in itself. She repeated the letters slowly until I gained confidence.

Sophie vocalised, 'M ... M ... M ... M.'
Un ... Um ... Am ... Em ... M

'Yes that's it. M.'

I struggled on valiantly. She taught me how to form simple words and eventually I developed a reading and talking age of a seven-year-old. The other staff thought she was mad for wasting her time on me as she often came in to sit with me on her days off. Mrs Tredegar, the owner, wasn't impressed.

'Why are you bothering with that senile fool when there are more worthy patients that deserve your attention. He'll be dead in a year or two so why bother?'

'The quantity of time he has on this earth is irrelevant when you place it alongside the quality. We can't leave him in a silent world when he's obviously quite intelligent. I'm sure he's been suffering from severe amnesia so just because he can't remember doesn't justify him being marginalised. '

'Well, if I find you neglecting the others I will have to reprimand you and perhaps even dismiss you which would be a shame as you are a good worker.'

'Don't worry I won't. I think it's time he started to mix and want to introduce him to the others at tea tomorrow.'

'I hope you know what you are doing. It will be your responsibility if things go wrong.'

'I'll make sure it doesn't.'

So the next day I was able to walk with Sophie's support into the lounge where a variety of men and women in their twilight years sat drinking tea and eating sandwiches. 'Hello,' I said brightly.

There was a general murmur of hellos and most returned to their eating although a couple gazed at me. One was an elderly lady who was smartly dressed, a single rope of pearls around her neck. The other looked like an academic with steel rimmed glasses and powdery grey hair. His jacket was worn thin with patches on his elbows.

'Come sit with me,' he beckoned, motioning me over to sit by his side. Fortunately I understood and moved to a grey armchair.

Sophie butted in, 'I'll get you some sandwiches and some tea and then I'll leave you to get to know everybody.'

'Do you play chess?' he asked.

'Chess?' I looked dismayed, as this was an unfamiliar word.

'Yes, you know. The board game.'

'Sorry I don't.'

'I'll teach you then. My name's Tom by the way. What's yours?'

'Sophie calls me Billy. I don't have another.'

'Oh well, Billy it is then. I'm glad you came and joined us as I heard you were locked away. Were you ill?'

'Not ill, exactly. Just learning how to live.'

'How odd. Did you have an accident or something?'

'Not sure what accident means. All I know is I can't remember.'

'Oh, it doesn't matter. I'll help show you the ropes anyway.'

'Ropes?'

'Just an expression. It means I'll show you round the place.'

'Oh' I said, still not entirely sure but willing to go along with it.

'Tomorrow OK?'

'Yes, OK.'

'Right now you've finished eating it's down to serious business. This is a chessboard . . . '

The next day I went with Tom around the grounds and he pointed out various places of interest.

'This is the pottery workshops, you know, bowls and stuff. Here is art therapy and over here is where the psychiatrists are based, psychos as I prefer to call them. I'm sure they'll ask to see you at some point.'

'I hope not.'

'We have a good gym, a swimming pool and tennis courts. Are your relatives paying for your upkeep?'

'I don't have any relatives.'

'Oh sorry, old chap. Well someone must have an interest in you.'

'Someone comes to see me once a month from the local council. I'm funded by a medical charity.'

'Must be an interesting case then.'

'I guess so. I wish I knew who I was.'

'You'll find out soon enough I'm sure.'

'I feel kind of odd somehow, not right,' I explained.

'You mean displaced somehow. Intriguing.'

'Can you recommend some books to read? I want to improve myself.'

'Of course. I'll take you to the library. I was a professor you know— English Lit and Philosophy. Unfortunately I kept on having blackouts and cant live on my own as it's pretty dangerous. Nearly died once. Still it's easy here. Plenty to do and no fuss. My daughter comes to see me once a month so I'm not totally isolated.'

And so began my quest for learning. I devoured everything that Tom gave me—working my way up from simple classics like The Little Prince until two years later I was working through Dostoevsky and A Brief History of Time. Sophie also guided me with education and general moral behaviour. 1 saw the psychos several times but none could fathom me out—they usually reached the wrong conclusions and still had no answers as to my identity. Hypnosis failed, as did other established therapies. No one could unlock the key to my past. One day I bumped into Sophie in the library.

'Billy, you're looking so much better,' Sophie remarked.

'I feel it.'

'You've got a sparkle in your eyes and you almost seem younger somehow. You were so hollow when you came in, now you're full of life.'

'I'm invigorated. I love to learn, almost thirst for it. I want to make up for what I've lost, to put something back.'

'You still don't have the faintest recollection?'

'No, I often wish for it but now I'm almost afraid. Perhaps it's better to start afresh—no matter how old I am or how long I have left.'

'You're certainly quick at learning. Brighter than most teenagers. And if you continue to improve healthwise, I reckon you've got a good few years left. You're always down the gym, putting the 60-year-olds to shame.'

'I hope so. I'd hate for it all to stop now it's getting so good. I'm really into philosophy and discovering myself through self analysis.'

'I see Mrs Sampson has persuaded you to attend the yoga class.'

'And meditation. I can relate a lot to Buddhism as I only recall the present so I can only live in the present. I'm free from all the baggage of past worries and failure.'

'That's the spirit. Be positive.'

'Oh I am. Through knowledge I can breathe. I've even beaten Tom at chess occasionally.'

'You have come so far in three years. You seemed so destroyed when I first met you.'

'I was lost and confused. Learning has given me a power over my life. Thanks to you and Tom I feel free.'

'That's great and more reward than anything else. Have you thought about moving to sheltered accommodation for more independence? I think you're ready.'

'I would like to but I don't want to leave Tom.'

'You could still visit. Talk it over with him.'

And so it was that I left the clinic for sheltered housing in Highgate. I felt great and settled into a comfortable life, living off a medical pension under the name of Billy Haylett. I spent my days going to the library, walking in the park and often visiting the clinic. My life changed again one day in the park. I was sitting on a bench reading a Borges book when a boy came up to me.

'Hello. Have you seen my cap anywhere? I left it on one of the benches but can't recall where.'

'No sorry,' I replied. 'What does it look like?'

'It's a baseball cap with "Broncos" written on it. Daddy brought it from the States.'

'Oh it must be extra special then. I often find when things are that special, they do turn up again.'

'I hope you're right. It was my favourite.'

'Do you play baseball?'

'No silly. They don't really play it here. Only rounders, which I think, is a sissy game. I like swimming best.'

'So do I. Do you go to the Highgate ponds to swim?'

'Sometimes. If the weather's nice. I prefer Swiss Cottage. You can go all year.'

'I've never been.'

'It's wonderful. They've got these new high diving boards and a jacuzzi. I'm going tomorrow with my sister. You can come if you like.'

'I'd love to. What's your name?'

'Jason. After *Jason and the Argonauts*. I'm ten next month.'

'My name's Billy.'

'You must be pretty old.'

'I'm not too sure how old I am. Somewhere in my seventies but it's all guesswork.'

'How silly not knowing how old you are.'

'I'm not sure it matters. It's how you feel that counts.'

'I feel hungry. I'd better go or Mum will be worried. I'm already late. I'll meet you at two outside Swiss Cottage tube. See you then.'

'See you. Bye.'

Meeting Jason was to give me a youthful vigour I had previously untapped. Up until then I had had little contact with children. He seemed so fresh, lively and yet innocent. I wondered if I was once the same. For a while that night I mourned my lost years but it was only momentary and I looked forward to the next day. Plus I had a special surprise for Jason.

'You found it.'

'It was under the bench at the end of the park. It must have fallen off.'

'Oh, thank you.'

I take it off my head where it lay perched awkwardly being much too small. He puts it on and runs off, returning when he remembers his manners.

'Oh, sorry, this is my sister Elspeth. Elsie for short.'

'Hello Elsie.'

'Hello Billy. Jason seems quite taken with you.'

'Really. We only met for five minutes. Still he seems a real live wire.'

'Come on,' says Jason. 'I want to get to the waterslides. They're fairly new.'

He runs off and we follow chatting.

'Are you still at school?'

'Yes, I'm 15. Taking my GCSEs at St Paul's. I'm taking nine subjects but I'm sure I'll fail Maths and Biology. I hate them.'

'What do you want to do after?'

'Oh I expect I'll take my As and then on to college. I want to study journalism.'

'Sounds fascinating. I'd love to have been a journalist.'

'What do you do then?'

'I'm medically retired now. I'm not sure what I used to do as I suffered chronic amnesia and can't remember anything apart from the past few years.'

'Oh how awful.'

'It has its compensations. I feel a lot like Jason as I have such a passion for everything new—a second childhood perhaps. Although I don't have the energy to run around physically, I chase ideas around my head all the time.'

'Here we are.' Jason tugs at my sleeve. 'It's pretty impressive isn't it.'

'Art Deco,' Elspeth adds. 'We studied that period last term.'

' I like what I've seen of Art Deco but I'm a mere amateur when it comes to art and architecture. I've just glimpsed through a few books in the library.'

'Stop chatting. Let's go in,' Jason pleads.

We spent a pleasant afternoon, the first of many, at the baths. They often invited me round for tea afterwards with their mother who was always considerate. We went to many other parks and attractions that summer and when term started we met up some weekends and holidays. Jason and Elspeth gave me new vision and added a dimension, which I could not obtain with study. One day, a year later, on my way to the clinic, I met up with Sophie outside.

'I'm sorry. I have some bad news for you,' she says. 'Tom died. A heart attack I'm afraid.'

'Oh no. I shall miss him, our chats and the games of chess. He was such a wise bird and an inspiration to me.'

'I know. We all will. Just be thankful it was quick and painless. He always said he would hate a lingering death.'

'I'm sure he would have done. Does his daughter know?'

'Yes. She is arranging the funeral. It's Thursday—you will come won't you?'

'Of course. Where is it?'

'St Neots just around the corner at two. We will have tea here afterwards.'

'I'll be there.'

'How are you anyway? You seem to look younger every time I see you.'

'My new young friends, Jason and Elspeth, keep me fit and often wear me out just keeping up with them.'

'A new elixir of life, hey?'

'You might be right, but still no memories.'

'I'd like to get Dr Houseman to give you a full medical next week if you, have time. Just want to make sure you are as fit as you look.'

'Of course. I'm sure he will find something the matter with me. Doctors always do.'

Tom's funeral was very sad and formal. His daughter Pam paid a lovely tribute to him and also thanked me for being a good friend. I promised to visit her soon to meet her husband. At the medical, Dr Houseman was impressed by my progress.

'Your body appears to be in good working order. Once the blood tests are back we'll know for certain. You have made excellent progress compared to when I first examined you four years ago.'

'I feel so much more alive. I was little more than a zombie when I first came here. Now I have developed a new lease of life and look forward to each day with glee.'

'I'm sure you'll have many more too. You are an encouraging sign to us all. I'm retiring next year. I hope I can maintain the same impetus.'

'I'm sure you will. You still play squash don't you?'

'Now and again. You don't play do you?'

'No I prefer to swim and work out in the gym four times a week.'

'Good for you. According to our records when you came in, we thought you were about seventy-five. I would now revise that figure by about eight to ten years. You appear to be closer to seventy.'

'It's amazing how contentment can roll back the years.'

'Too true. You are a flagship for this clinic. Perhaps you would like to come to talk to some of the newer patients about your experiences. You might help them to adjust.'

'I would be proud and honoured.'

'I'll get Sophie to contact you with a suitable day.'

'I'd better get something prepared.'

It was odd having my position at the clinic reversed from one of patient to educator yet I leapt at the challenge with relish. It was there that I was to perhaps grasp at a new concept I had not previously considered. Emily was the one to raise it. In the group comments after my talk, she admitted she had gone into catatonic shock after the death of her son and had only after two years begun to function reasonably well. Yet her mind often relapsed when any departure from routine occurred. I suspected it was an example of post traumatic stress disorder having read up on the subject in an attempt to discover if I had suffered something similar, Sophie had recommended it.

'I can't really accept what has happened. It is as if my mind has gone into reverse. I seem to be clawing back the years before Michael's death and cannot adjust to the present,' she said.

'Well in some ways I can relate to that,' I replied. 'I think my body has gone into reverse as I seem to be getting younger since whatever happened to make me lose my memory occurred. I am unsure if it is a lack of worry over the past as I have none or some other coping mechanism. Perhaps my whole system is going in reverse.'

It was only when I articulated this that I realise I was only saying what had lain dormant in my mind for the past year now. Was it true that I was really going back in age or did I just feel that way? Perhaps no conception of the past enabled us all to do this. After all Emily in her own way was emulating this in her mind. Was it possible to do this physically as well? I had to find out. I had to see someone. I booked an appointment with a doctor at St Thomas's who was an expert on age and its effects on the body. His name was Dr Hansard.

'Do you think I am mad, doctor, for believing this.'

'Not necessarily. You certainly seem, according to the records Dr Houseman sent me, to be reversing the age process somehow. Whether you were affected by the trauma, which led you to lose your memory, and this caused you to temporarily age rapidly, which was subsequently reversed upon you starting your life afresh, is uncertain. Perhaps memory does play a role in ageism. I have uncovered a few similar cases before but none that are so extreme. I would like to carry out some tests in the course of a year to find out if the physical process is really in retrograde.'

'I will consent to anything if it clears this up. I would really like to know. Do you think writing a book would be a good idea as it might help me to understand certain things?'

'Yes I do. It could go alongside the examinations.'

And so I began this tale you are now reading. After a year of tests the results came back. Physically, I was getting younger. What had caused this to happen? I am now about to embark on some serious research of my own to ascertain the truth. When I have found this out I will finish this story but for now I will leave you here so that you have the option whether to discover the secret of reversing time. You may want to join me on my travels against the power of nature. Can I blow the whole Darwinian myth single-handed? If you have the courage to find out, you will wait a few years. Come take your life into your own hands and follow me.

Winding Back © Clare Barstow 2000

Changing History is by **Ralf Bolden,** an African-American who grew up in Colorado. He tells us that he discovered sailing while studying languages at University in Europe and as a yachtmaster, he spent 20 years sailing over 100,000 nautical miles while circumnavigating the planet with his wife Jeannette Dean. Both are serving nine years imprisonment in England. When released, they plan to sail around the world again and to continue writing fiction and feature articles.

Ralf Bolden's work has been published in *Prison Writing, Inside Time, Sunday Independent, New Impact Journal, Sci-Fright, Writing for Television, Strix* and *Voyage Magazine.* He has recently earned a University Diploma in European Humanities from the Open University.

Changing History

Ralf Bolden

Tom's coffee-coloured skin looked healthy in the stark light of the mahogany-panelled courtroom. He sat reading *The Time Machine* while his twin brother Jamie did the talking.

'You don't understand,' said Jamie shifting nervously in the dock. 'You are offering us the choice between freedom and liberty.'

'How so?' the red-robed English judge asked, scratching his wig with one hand and taking notes with the other.

'You've never sailed with sperm whales off Sri Lanka, traded with tribesman in New Guinea, danced with Tahitians on Moorea or walked with giant tortoises in the Galapagos. To us that's freedom,' said Jamie wetting his lips. 'Liberty is what the State offers its citizens provided they don't break the rules. If we comply with your confiscation order and surrender our assets, we'll lose our freedom to gain liberty. That's unacceptable.'

The judge peered over his pince-nez spectacles with azure-blue eyes and asked, 'Do you refuse to sign the power-of-attorney Mr. Jamie Heart?'

'Yeah,' Jamie said in a broad Caribbean accent.

'I assume that like your brother you too refuse to co-operate, Mr. Tom Heart?'

Tom put down *The Time Machine* and said, 'That's right.' He wore a white T-shirt, blue jeans and deck shoes with the muscular body of a weight lifter. His Afro-Caribbean hair was cut short to accent deep-set golden eyes. The fragrant smell of his vanilla after-shave wafted across the courtroom.

'I have no choice. I am going to make an order allowing the Receivers to sign the documents on your behalf. You are in contempt of court with no respect for our laws,' said the judge sneering. 'And you're going to find out this court has teeth. Take them down.'

Sitting below in the court's cells, Jamie composed a letter to his wife:

'Dearest Love of My Life, You looked absolutely splendid at court. The feel of your kiss in the hallway when we were being taken back to the cells will remain with me forever. Today in court, we didn't understand the legal goings on and we weren't allowed legal representation but the prosecution was. Yet, the judge said, we were going to find out this court has teeth. I am perplexed. If a British court has the power to sign over the assets of foreign nationals in extra-territorial jurisdictions why bully us into committing an offence like contempt? Call you on Saturday. I love you with all my heart, Jamie.'

He re-read the letter, placed it in an envelope, and fell asleep with his head against the window of the van taking them back to prison.

When Jamie and Tom returned to their cell they found a small crumpled man, wrapped in a green prison blanket, hooded like a desert tribesman. He was sitting on the third bed in the already cramped conditions watching Sky TV. The cell was a cream-coloured box four meters by two meters with a desk, three chairs and a window. A toilet and sink were in the corner. Illumination was provided by a single fluorescent light situated in the middle of the three metre high ceiling.

'Hi,' Tom said, trying to be a friendly as possible.

'Hello,' said the crumpled figure in a refined English voice, his grey eyes alert. 'Sorry for the intrusion but I was put in here.'

Jamie held out his hand. 'My name is Jamie Heart and this is my brother Tom.'

'My name is Vaughn Three.' He extended a blistered three-fingered hand from under the blanket. Jamie shook it quickly then unconsciously wiped his hand on his jeans.

Tom asked, 'Care for a cup of tea?' He sensed Vaughn's stare. It followed their every movement with curious detachment like they were being studied. Vaughn said, 'I'm not supposed to be in here.'

'We all say that,' Jamie said, stirring his tea.

'Don't mind him,' said Tom. 'He's always a bit sarcastic.'

Vaughn looked at each of them intently then asked, 'What year is it?'

'It's 2020,' Jamie said, staring at the hooded man, 'why?'

In a clear voice Vaughn Three said, 'I'd hoped it would be 2090.'

'No way, it's 2020 all right,' interrupted Jamie. 'Why are you in jail anyway?'

'The police arrested me in Cambridge when I tried to change some gold bars into money. The shopkeeper said I was acting suspiciously.'

'They can do that now. Arrest anyone and confiscate their assets without a warrant if you can't prove how you got them,' said Tom, his muscular-brown torso propped up against the cell's wall. 'We're yachtsmen and hash smugglers so they know where we got ours. What about you?'

'I'm from the future. I brought the gold with me to support myself while I showed them my mathematical proof on the existence of God.'

'What kind of defence is that?' Tom asked.

Jamie almost rolled off the top bunk laughing. 'Hey Vaughn, you didn't really believe that would work did you?'

Vaughn Three shifted position on the bed, covered his drooping shoulder with the prison blanket and grasped his blue-plastic mug of tea with two three-fingered hands. He drank and said, 'Today is June thirteenth. At six o'clock the Association of Southeast Asian Nations will announce they've tested a nuclear device. Go on, turn on the news.'

'OK Vaughn, we can take a joke,' Tom said, switching the channel. They sat in silence waiting for the hourly news. The bells of Big Ben sounded and the announcer said, 'The Association of Southeast Asian Nations have just tested a nuclear device.'

'Wow, that was impressive,' said Tom. 'How did you know?'

'I have a photographic memory,' said Vaughn. 'I've studied every detail of this century to find the exact moment in history to avert the nuclear holocaust. Only I landed in 2020 instead of 2090.'

'Wait a minute,' said Jamie sceptically. 'This is jail, know what I mean. In here, you're always assaulted with tissues of lies.'

'Here is a clipping from a newspaper of my time. You'll notice the difference in the texture of the newsprint. It's synthetic.'

Jamie grabbed the cutting and read it aloud, 'It's from *Who's-Who*. The Biography of Vaughn Three: Born at the end of the nuclear holocaust in 2099 and horribly disfigured by genetic mutation, Vaughn Three grew up in a sanctuary run by The Earth Corporation. He excelled in mathematics and proved the existence of God with a brilliant extrapolation of the Hawkins Theory of Cosmology. He was Professor Emeritus of Mathematics at Microsoft University in Cambridge until he uncovered the secrets of temporal mechanics. His goal is to travel back in time before the holocaust to show them he'd proved: God is love.'

Throwing the clipping oh the bed next to Vaughn, Jamie said, 'What a bunch of crap. If you're from the future, why don't you just teleport out of here?'

'The police confiscated my watch,' said Vaughn Three, slumping over. 'The device was hidden in my watch.'

'And you can't get your watch back until you get out of here.' said Jamie looking at Tom.

'And you can't get out of here,' said Tom, 'until you pay the fine for the confiscation order.'

'That's it,' Vaughn said.

'We're in the same situation,'' said Jamie. 'Except we refuse to satisfy the order because we think it's wrong to get multiple punishments for the same crime.'

'Yeah,' said Tom. 'We got one sentence for the hash. When that's done we got another for the money and another on top of that for not paying the money. I hate this system.'

'Me too,' said Jamie. 'It's corrupt. One law for the wealthy and one for the common man.'

'I hated them for busting us,' said Tom. 'What's a little hash?'

'A man's got to have a good smoke. Even if it was two tonnes,' said Jamie. 'I mean it's better than alcohol. Who ever heard of a bloke going home to beat up his wife after having a joint?' The Caribbean brothers nodded in agreement.

'One day you'll be vindicated,' said Vaughn, smiling under the hood formed by his blanket. 'But only after the world has been disseminated by nuclear war. Cannabinoids are the only thing that can alleviate the suffering of mutants like me.'

'Is that why you're covered up like a Bedouin?' Tom asked. Vaughn Three unwrapped the green blanket. Tom ran to the toilet and retched. Vaughn's skin had enlarged white pores that looked like tiny scales. He had thin-pink lips and grey eyes. His eyebrows and scalp were bald. The boils on his neck seemed to slowly grow yellow pimples and burst with tiny larvae as they watched. 'Don't mind them. They eat the cancerous flesh,' he said. One lycra-covered leg was a good twenty centimetres shorter than the other. He looked like a twisted gnome out of a fairy tale by the Brothers Grimm.

Vaughn Three covered himself up again. 'Nuclear war is the menace,' he said. 'It must be stopped.'

Tom came back and sat on the lower bunk next to Jamie after flushing the toilet with bleach to kill the smell.

'How did the nuclear war start?' Jamie asked.

'In the middle of this century, Serbia became the dominant-economic power in central Europe and they acquired nuclear weapons,' Vaughn explained, sipping his tea. 'They bombed Macedonia, breaking the UN mandate. NATO satellites fired lasers on Belgrade, Serbia's Slavic neighbours retaliated against the West and in six months time the atmosphere was rich in nuclear waste. People were forced to live underground in the old mines from Cornwall to Mansfield. Only the Earth Corporation colonies on the moon and Mars were unaffected.' Then Vaughn Three said, 'I have a plan but I need your help.'

'What might that be?' Jamie asked, shaking his head. 'I have a feeling I'm not going to like this.'

'Let's hear him out,' said Tom. 'It won't hurt to listen.'

'I'm going to court next week,' said Vaughn Three. 'To have my assets confiscated, get a fine and a jail sentence in lieu if I can't pay the fine.'

'We'll all be up on the same day,' said Tom. 'The Confiscation Court only sits on Wednesdays.'

'So what's your plan?' Jamie asked.

Slowly Vaughn explained, 'You sign over your assets and get out of jail because I imagine you've still got something hidden away.' There was a long pause. 'I'll feed you information about what stocks to buy when you come visit me.'

'Then what?' Jamie asked.

'When there's enough money, you pay my fine and we'll be partners,' explained Vaughn. 'Remember, I have a photographic memory and know what has already happened in this century. With, our wealth, we may be able to redirect history and avert the nuclear holocaust.'

'But if we do succeed and change history, will you cease to exist?' Jamie asked, having already read *The Time Machine*.

'Vaughn smiled knowingly and said, 'If that's the price I must pay to avert a nuclear war, it's for the best.'

Tom looked at Jamie and said, 'Why not? We may get rich.'

Jamie said, 'We've taken bigger risks than this. If it works we'll be able to get our revenge on the system.'

Vaughn extended his three-fingered hand in partnership. Jamie and Tom looked at each other, shrugged their shoulders and shook his hand.

●　　●　　●

The Corporate Three became the wealthiest firm in the world. It held over thirty per cent of the planet's wealth and fought for the end of nuclear proliferation, multiple punishments for the same crime, the marijuana laws, arrest without a warrant and also the end of The Nanny State. At a televised speech in front of the United Nations to celebrate the destruction of the last nuclear weapons, the hooded figure of Sir Vaughn Three shuffled about, explaining his mathematical proof on the existence of God when he vanished from the screen.

'There will be no funeral,' said Jamie at the press conference afterwards. Tears flowed down his cheek as he spoke. 'Tom and I knew Vaughn Three for over 30 years and we'd like to leave you with a quote from his favourite book written in the Age of Enlightenment by Voltaire: 'All is for the best, in this best of all possible worlds'.'

Changing History © Ralf Bolden 2000

A round-up of recently published books . . .

Walking Away, Hugh Collins, Canongate, £10 (Paperback)

Shortly after his release from a life sentence in 1993, Hugh Collins published the widely acclaimed *Autobiography of a Murderer*. A compelling book, written in the same way that Collins speaks, it covered his life in the Glasgow gangs of the 1960s and 70s, leading up to the killing of a rival and the sixteen years he spent in prison. Transferred to the Barlinnie Special Unit after he stabbed three prison officers in Perth, Collins found therapeutic relief in sculpture, but his real catharsis has come through writing.

Walking Away is a further attempt to exorcise not only the murder he committed, but a lifetime of unresolved business. Many lifers come out with a heavy burden of emotional baggage; Collins carries more than most. The demons that pervaded his first book still lurk; the expectations of family and friends almost suffocate him; the fears within him are quelled temporarily by illegal opiates, only to exacerbate the guilt that will not leave him.

Much of *Walking Away* covers the period during which Collins wrote his first book. Rage pours forth as his past flashes back, to juxtapose with the present—a demanding and unreasonable mother, an anti-hero father who rejects him, the hectoring and pretentiousness of a prison visitor whom he feels still looks on him only as a murderer, antipathy towards his old mentor Jimmy Boyle, everyone asking the same question—'How do you feel?', lack of money—and a prison system that ejected him after 16 years and expected him to set up a new, law-abiding life with only forty pounds in his pocket. The only person who escapes unscathed from Collins' rage is his wife, the painter Caroline McNairn, whose faith in him never wavers no matter what crisis or tragedy looms. But Collins' angst is directed mostly at himself, as the man he once was fights with the man he now must be, indeed wants to be.

From its beginning with Collins coming out of prison, to its unexpected ending, *Walking Away* captivates. The three year period that it covers sees Collins slowly starting to become easier with life outside, of him finally being allowed to grow as a person rather than stagnate as a criminal or prisoner, of the past being slowly pushed back. His honesty, ironic humour, the spare but vivid prose and the exquisite use of dialect make this a classic work of autobiography, regardless of genre.

Mr Blue: Memoirs of a Renegade, Edward Bunker, No Exit Press, £7.99 (Paperback)

Edward Bunker, the man of the moment in American crime fiction, and a former interviewee in *Prison Writing*, was the youngest ever inmate of San Quentin. *Mr Blue*, the title of these memoirs, was the part he played in the movie 'Reservoir Dogs'. Along the way he wrote four novels that have become essential reading for those who like a writer who's *been there*. Bunker certainly has been there and in *Mr Blue* he tells the story of his life in the same way that he writes his novels—tight, flowing prose that brims with insights into the criminal psyche and gives leading clues as to the origins of his characters and story lines.

Mr Blue is no mere criminal autobiography. Bunker might have once been on the FBI's 'Most Wanted' list and served all those years in California's worst penitentiaries, but he is a writer through and through, one who writes about crime from the criminal's viewpoint. Meeting Caryl Chessman, the San Quentin inmate who penned *Cell 2455 Death Row*, gave him his start and he never looked back, although he had to sell his blood to post his manuscripts to an agent and in seventeen years he wrote six unpublished novels before *No Beast So Fierce* was accepted.

Bunker pays only fleeting mention at the end of his book to his successful years. *Mr Blue* is about his source material: his childhood, the only son of a Hollywood stagehand and a chorus girl; the tearaway teenage years in children's homes and military schools; the vivid and violent realities of life in prison, and the characters he came across before he decided once and for all to lay down the gun and pick up the pen. His was a life lived on the very edge of American society, a hard life and a hard struggle to succeed: He writes: 'The traits that made me fight the world are those that allowed me to prevail.' As four novels, an Oscar nomination for a screenplay and acting appearances in a score of films prove, Edward Bunker has prevailed.

Dead Run, Joe Jackson and William Burke Jnr, Canongate, £10 (Paperback)

Dead Run is a fast paced account of the only mass escape from any Death Row in America; an account of a legal system that kills people who are invariably black and poor, on the flimsiest of evidence, and of Dennis Stockton, a petty but persistent criminal who spent twelve years on Death Row in Mecklenburg Prison, Virginia before meeting his judicial doom in 1995.

When the escape was planned Stockton was invited along, but he declined, pinning his faith on an appeal that he believed would quash his murder conviction. Instead, he logged in a diary the events leading up to the escape by six of his fellow inmates and it is this diary, plus a column he wrote for a state newspaper, that forms the basis of *Dead Run*. Impeccably researched, the book is written in a style that maintains suspense all through the escape and its repercussions, through Stockton's fight to avoid the death penalty, the decision he had to make regarding the electric chair or lethal injection, to his last breath. The manner in which the authors detail the characters and tensions of death row existence—with its brutality, boredom, and grim humour, set in a web of official corruption and negligence—makes this a remarkable book.

The Pain and the Pride: Life Inside the Colorado Boot Camp, Brian P. Block, Waterside Press, £10 (Paperback)

Boot camps evoke an image of military prisons for juveniles, all square-bashing, shouting and polishing parade grounds. Brian P. Block, an English magistrate, spent two weeks at Buena Vista boot camp in Colorado and his book describes a rather different regime. The boot camp sentence is one of three months, most of the inmates are illiterate and all are there as part of a sentence much longer than they would be likely to get for a similar offence in Britain. While the programme does involve what is referred to as 'traditional corrections', discipline and physical fitness, there is a great deal of input on education—literacy, parenting, drug and alcohol, and cognitive exercises.

The ethos is 'We cannot change you, but you can change yourselves'. Instructors give no credence to the belief held by many offenders that it is they who are victims. At Buena Vista the inmates' pasts cannot be changed, but their futures can. Nor is blaming bad company an acceptable excuse for getting into trouble—a sign on the wall reads 'Who is the wrong crowd? We are the wrong crowd'

Cost, of course, plays a significant part. Boot camps in the US (though not the YOI based on a similar model at Thorn Cross, Cheshire) are cheaper to run than ordinary prisons and recidivism rates are lower. Thirty five per cent of boot camp 'graduates' are re-convicted within three years, compared to over sixty percent for ex-prisoners over the whole of the USA.

The author's documentary approach works well. He's seen what goes on and his writing style shares the fly-on-the-wall experience with the reader.

Bronson, Charles Bronson with Robin Ackroyd, Blake, £14.99 (Hardback)

Prison Writing's link with Charles Bronson goes back to the very first issue, in 1992, when we printed an extract from his unpublished autobiography, *Insanity Drove Me Mad*. The manuscript, written in Bronson's own hand, much of it in capitals which at times gave it the effect of being shouted from a prison roof, chronicled his odyssey through the punishment blocks and special hospitals of the English criminal justice system. Heavy with violence—done to him and done by him in roughly equal measures—it also abounded with a surreal sense of humour that showed another side of his troubled personality.

Insanity Drove Me Mad never saw the light of day, which was a pity, if only for the loss of a wonderful title. Instead, Bronson published a volume of poems and cartoons, an autobiography last year titled *Silent Scream*, and now this one, which, although ghosted, appears to be the 'official' version, as far as one can tell.

Bronson—born Michael Peterson—has had a lifelong quest to prove something to the rest of the world. As a young petty criminal he would always go one step further than his friends; as a prisoner for most of the past twenty six years he has bowed to no one, with the end result that at the age of almost 50 he is more disturbed than ever. One of the few prisoners to be held in Broadmoor, Rampton and Ashworth special hospitals, he was discharged back into the prison system when a tribunal could not decide why he had been sectioned, seven years earlier. 'I'd been certified mad because of my violence. I was still violent – and they were now certifying me sane. Where's the sanity in that?'

His book is a catalogue of hostage taking, stabbings and beatings. Constantly on the move from seg block to seg block, often waking up not being able to remember where he was—in actual time he must have served months of his sentences on the motorways. Yet for all the violence and braggadocio, Bronson is clearly an emotional man who has a surprising amount of insight into his actions and what triggers them. He also, very unusually in a book written by a disruptive prisoner, gives credit to a number of prison officers and even the odd probation officer.

Bronson is proud of his reputation as a difficult prisoner – this is understandable for it is all he possesses. But here lies the dilemma—if he were able to behave himself for a significant period, he would then become an ordinary prisoner. Reading his book, one gets the impression that would not be enough to sustain the forces that drive him.

Jackrabbit Parole, Stephen Reid, McArthur and Company, Toronto $8.99 (Paperback)

Jackrabbit Parole, American jail-slang for escape, has a cartoon quality which reflects the strange unreality of life as a professional bank robber. Originally published in 1986, the novel has been re-issued, presumably to coincide with the latest phase of Stephen Reid's alternating career pattern: robber-writer- robber.

Reid was serving a 16 year sentence, when the manuscript for *Jackrabbit Parole* came into the hands of Susan Musgrave, poet and University writer-in-residence. She fell in love, 'not with the idea of a glamorous bank robber . . . but with words, which is what I always fall in love with, anyone who can write'. Her publisher shared her enthusiasm and when Reid was released the book was published. They had already married, while he was still in prison. He settled into a long spell of domesticity and quasi-respectability, as Canada's answer to Edward Bunker. The pair became darlings of the literary in-crowd and Reid made a living from writing and running workshops, on both sides of the wall. But he never managed to extricate himself from his long-standing heroin addiction. In June 1999, wearing an Elvis mask and a policeman's uniform, Reid went back to bank robbery.

Jackrabbit Parole is a compelling and entertaining tale of the life and times of a

7

bank-robbing gang, with all the bickering, adrenalin-surge and bravado of the heist, followed by triumph and anti-climax: suitcases full of cash and an urgent need to disappear. Women are left at home—decorative and sexy, well provided for, but inevitably wanting more out of a relationship than a bank robber can offer—'All I ever wanted was a cold beer and a warm welcome. Lately she had it backward.'

The novel has all the ugly drama of real crime, told by someone who has lived it. We follow the gang through the crime itself, on to high living, more plotting, betrayal, justice, prison, a spectacular break-out, and a complicated twisty ending involving a renegade cop. His problem is an excess of moral fervour: hence he fouls things up for everyone else, both cops and robbers. 'The general consensus on a top-priority arrest like ours is to shoot until everyone is dead and let God sort it out . . . But there is the odd joker in the deck, an idealist of sorts.' If Reid has it right, criminals can perhaps comfort themselves with the notion that the forces of law and order are almost as amoral as they are.

Earlier this year, soon after Stephen Reid was sentenced to 18 years imprisonment, the *Toronto Globe and Mail* announced that he had been lined up to provide a weekly column. A deluge of letters to the editor from outraged readers put paid to that plan. At least he should have time to produce more books.

Mad Frank's Diary: A Chronicle of the Life of Britain's Most Notorious Villain, Frankie Fraser with James Morton, Virgin, £16.99 (Hardback)

Following on from his two volumes of memoirs, *Mad Frank's Diary* is not a day by day journal of the author's life, more a collection of reminiscences and opinions on what happened on particular dates in the calendar. So, in the first entry we find 1 January 1984—'New Year's always a sad time because it was then Billy Hill died in 1984 in his flat in Moscow Road in Bayswater.' Moving on to 10 March 1965, it gets a little more personal— 'Of course,

there was always a chance I'd be topped. It was unlikely. First, I'd got to be found guilty and then it was going to be a bit difficult seeing that I'd been certified as mad twice.' Or, 17 December 1990—'There's always something good about seeing a bent copper go down. The trouble is it doesn't happen often enough.' You get the idea . . .

Unlike many of his contemporaries, whom he takes to task for not always living their lives by his code, he does not indulge in sensation or hyperbole—rather he is a master of sinister understatement. Acts of the most extreme violence are recounted quite matter of fact: in an entry headed August Bank Holiday, writing of an acquaintance named Happy Sambridge—'although he wasn't when I'd finished with him'—who had done him an earlier disservice, he says: 'I caught up with him years later . . . Someone marked my card where he was in London and I took his leg off with a shotgun.' Or how about this for a family anecdote, Fraser style . . . 9 November 1980, writing of his niece: 'This was a bad day for the family. Poor Shirley, Eva's daughter, got nicked for murder. The coppers came round one Sunday and there was a man's head on a plate in her fridge. Just like John the Baptist.'

As it says on the back cover—'Mad Frankie Fraser's memories are like your worst nightmares. You'd want them to stay in the past. But Frankie wants to share . . .' In today's popular culture, the market for living anti-heroes is buoyant. Fraser's books sell because he is the real article—fully certified (twice, as he points out), decades of bird behind him and utterly unrepentant.

Lord Longford's Prison Diary, Edited by Peter Stanford, Lion Publishing, £14.99 (Hardback)

For almost 65 years Frank Longford has visited prisons. Even now, at the age of ninety five, his stooped and shuffling gait is a familiar sight in visiting rooms up and down the country. He has faced criticism and ridicule with equanimity for befriending prisoners but few of those who have dismissed him as a 'crank' have ever tried to understand him. Similarly, the general opinion that he is only interested in high profile prisoners is a false one—as will be seen in the pages of this book. For every Nilsen and Hindley there are dozens of others whom the general public will never have heard of.

This is a diary of Longford's prison visits from 1995 to 1999. Interspersed are a few snapshot entries from his 'outside' life. Thus, thrown in alongside trips to Wandsworth and Whitemoor, we find a lunch at Windsor Castle where he sits between the Queen and Princess Anne. But mostly it is an account which anyone who visits prisons regularly will identify with—the only surprise is that a man who is peer of the realm, Knight of the Garter and an ex-cabinet minister has to put up with the same sort of nonsense as ordinary folk. The obstructions, delays and diversionary tactics employed by prison bureaucracy feature throughout the diary, but the overwhelming impression is of a man who feels it is his duty to visit prisoners and to take up their cases and causes.

Lord Longford is driven by a belief that prison can reform and redeem criminals. To this end he campaigns tirelessly, writing to prison service officials and ministers—and with a surprising number of positive outcomes as his diary shows. The entries also raise many questions about his attitude to crime and punishment in general, which the editor attempts to resolve by including a question and answer sequence at the end of the book.

Grendon: The History of a Therapuetic experiment, Bob Healey, with a Foreword by Martin Narey (Free to visitors to HMP Grendon. Not for sale).

Books on the history of individual prisons are not unusual, but one written by a current inmate most certainly is. Published to celebrate forty years of sustaining the therapeutic community idea at HMP Grendon—the East-Hubert Report of 1939 laid down the foundations for the prison, which eventually opened in 1962—the author, Bob Healey, has done a fine job in researching and writing this account, from the earliest days to the present.

Grendon caters for prisoners who are in need of therapy and willing to co-operate. Here, its work is shown in the context of the overall prison estate, its regime, assessment and admission procedures revealed, and its rehabilitative programmes explained. Most people who visit Grendon—especially on one of the frequent open days—come away wondering why there are not more such establishments in the British penal system. Bob Healey has written a lively book (as befits an author whose work has appeared in *Prison Writing*!) which should be read by every politician or official who has a responsibility for penal policy.

Drug Treatment In Prison

An Evaluation of the RAPt Treatment Programme
CAROL MARTIN and ELAINE PLAYER
The findings of a two-year study into the effectiveness of the RAPt drug treatment programme which enables male prisoners with self-confessed problems of substance misuse to lead a drug and alcohol-free life in prison and in the community after release. The report also assesses whether completion of the programme is associated with a reduction in the likelihood of reconviction post-release. A unique and highly significant collection of information and data. 96 pages ISBN 1 872 870 26 0 **£10** plus £2 p&p (Europe £3; elswhere £6).

Prison(er) Education

STORIES OF CHANGE AND TRANSFORMATION
Edited by **David Wilson and Anne Reuss**

The first major collection of writings about the transforming power of education in British prisons. Key essays by leading prison education practitioners, academics and prisoners, *Prison(er) Education* include new work on how to evaluate the 'success' of education within prison by Dr Ray Pawson of Leeds University, and Stephen Duguid of Simon Fraser University, Canada. A serving lifer describes the impact of education on his time inside, and two of the UK's leading prison educationalists at HMP Whitemoor describe their work and it's power to transform. New research from the archives of the Prisoners Education Trust is presented by Emma Hughes. 192 pages ISBN 1 872 870 90 2. £18 plus £2 p&p (Europe £3; elsewhere £6).

A major challenge to penal policy-makers to accept the value of education - beyond 'basic skills', and at a time when regimes have come to be dominated by cognitive thinking skills courses.

Edited by Professor David Wilson of the University of Central England (a former prison governor and co-presenter of BBC TV's 'Crime Squad'), and **Dr Anne Reuss** of the University of Abertay Dundee (who previously taught at HM Prison Full Sutton). The editors also write introductory and concluding chapters.

Weaving anecdote, research and evaluation this book presents a comprehensive account of education inside British prisons and asks: 'Who is prison(er) education for - prison or prisoner?'

Prison on Trial
SECOND ENGLISH EDITION (2000)

This edition of *Prison On Trial* contains all six original chapters plus a new *Foreword* and *Preface,* and a substantial *Postcript* by the author. There is also an extended *Bibliography* and a new *Index.*

Prison On Trial distils the arguments for and against imprisonment in a readable, accessible and authoritative way – making Thomas Mathiesen's work a classic for students and other people concerned to understand the real issues. It is as relevant today as when it was first published – arguably more so as policy-making becomes increasingly politicized and true opportunities to influence developments diminish. Mindful of this, Mathiesen recommends an 'alternative public space' where people can engage in valid discussion on the basis of sound information, free from the survival priority of the media – to entertain. *Prison On Trial* has been influential in many jurisdictions. It has already been published in **Norwegian, Danish, Swedish, German, English** and **Spanish** – and it is currently being translated into **Italian.** £19.50 plus £2 p&p (Europe £3; elsewhere £6)

Scheduled for March 2001

Grendon Tales
STORIES FROM A THERAPEUTIC COMMUNITY
Ursula Smartt

Weaving first-hand accounts by members of HM Prison Grendon's therapuetic 'communities' and staff with personal research and observation, Ursula Smartt takes readers behind the scenes at one of the UK's best-known and forward-looking prisons. Her analysis of 'the Grendon experience' goes beyond straightforward description of this world famous establishment to examine the shifts (subtle and not so subtle), tensions and possibilities which underpin day-to-day life and the process of change in offenders. *Grendon Tales* is a powerful, scholarly and readable work which is destined to become a lasting tribute to this unique establishment on its fortieth anniversary in 2001. ISBN 1 872 870 96 1. Price £18 plus £2 p&p (Europe £3; elsewhere £6)

WATERSIDE PRESS • DOMUM ROAD • WINCHESTER • SO23 9NN
Full catalogue /Orders: ☎ Tel/fax 01962 855567
E-mail: watersidepress@compuserve.com
Or visit www.watersidepress.co.uk – to view over 100 Waterside titles.